Breaking through the Barriers of Success

How to Explode your Business Growth with only 6 simple strategies, YOU can employ today!

Written by:
Tevon Coney with MJ

D1361826

First Printing Edition, 2022
ISBN   9798360705185

Printed in The United States of America

"Would you like me to give you a formula for success? It's quite simple, really: Double your rate of failure. You are thinking of failure as the enemy of success. But it isn't at all. You can be discouraged by failure, or you can learn from it, so go ahead and make mistakes. Make all you can. Because remember that's where you will find success." — *Thomas J. Watson*

Table of Contents

"Any fool can know. The point is to understand." — *Albert Einstein*

For more information or get involved with us reach out to Jan Capital Inc. www.jancapitalinc.com

Dedication

Mom and dad, you're the reason I'm authoring this book. You taught me all about breaking through the barriers of success. Oftentimes we focus on our goals that we want to accomplish in life and when adversity occurs, we must respond.

Growing up and understanding the importance of never to give up despite the circumstances and constantly finding creative ways to improve yourself or your business. At this moment you have either read just the front cover and now reading this dedication page or you have read the front/back and now reading this wondering what this book about is and how do you break through the barriers of success. One thing I have learned early in my career thus far is that there are a million ways to do one single thing in business, so my advice would be to become more creative and find the problem and solve the solution. Which is a repeated cycle but offers you the ability to always find a way to break the barriers that you're facing.

Eventually, you begin to enjoy solving simple and complex problems because your brain develops the mental capacity to expand and create in several ways to solve the problem that may be keeping your business from going to the next level.

Our barriers are not as complicated that we often make it seem as but it's more so giving our brain the opportunity to expand like it knows best. I want to thank both of my parents for the way they raised me to view adversity as an opportunity to gain experience and not a setback. I can think back to the instances where I ran into barriers in both my personal and business life and reverted to the tools that my parents had given me to use when I felt like there was a roadblock that occurred in my life. The "why" you're doing something was a major tool I used as motivation to push through many circumstances.

The focus is improving and creating multiple ways to be successful at what you're doing in your career. There is no right or wrong way to do things and writing my first book was to inform many that success comes in many ways and make your own definition of what you define success as.

What do you consider success? Think about that and write it down in your journal and create a plan in your business that helps you build to that ultimate level you want to reach. My parents made me do that exercise at the age of about 10 years old and that one tool I use to this day as motivation, and I want to show my parents how much I love and thank them for their guidance and giving me the tools to break through the barriers to success. Thank you to my mom Cloette and my dad Timothy, I want to make you proud.

Breaking through the Barriers of Success

How to Explode your Business Growth with only 6 simple strategies, YOU can employ today!

BY TEVON CONEY WITH MJ

Chapter 1

SELL YOUR BUSINESS FOR THE MOST AMOUNT $$$

"So often people are working hard at the wrong thing. Working on the right thing is probably more important than working hard." — Caterina Fake

PREPARE

The same principles and strategies work whether you are selling a dying business or one that is on the upswing. Valuations obviously vary, but the real valuation is, "what is the amount that you would accept for your business?" You can listen to all the discussions about multiples, assets and on and on, but the people who are going to sell a 10-million-dollar company are not reading this book and learning the strategies. Small business owners either must pass the business down the family line or must have an exit strategy. A business or anything is only worth what someone will pay for it.

Selling can be an exciting time, but it can be a bittersweet moment because you're getting rid of something you put so much demanding work into. At the same time, it's an opportunity for you to decide what to do with your fortunes and enjoy it. If one is at the stage where they're in the process of selling or have enough cash flow and equity to sell but may not be sure exactly how. Connecting with people like myself, MJ and others will give your insight on just how easy it is to get what your business is worth and more because of all your efforts to get the business established and profitable. Those are two areas that often get overlooked but, they're the most important for all levels of business owners. I think back to the process that got my first business acquired in under 3 years but one of the key components of the deal was how impressive our balance sheet was. Having your expenses and profits in order is mandatory when approaching one about buying your business. Of course, there are people on the market that are looking to buy companies and take them to the next level. The important part is to ask yourself is my business structure properly for someone to pay you for your book of business and product. If the answer is yes, then that's a wonderful spot to be in because your time is coming. If the answer is no, that's fine we just have more work to do.

In addition, when you're looking to sell, ask yourself how much you are willing to take. Sometimes buyers will be fair and give you exactly what your business is worth but on the other hand you have predators that are ready to take your business over for cheap and turn it into a profitable machine. I have seen it more times than not where a business owner doesn't understand the actual value they have and end up giving the business for much less than it's worth. As a current business owner, I dislike seeing that occur because I understand the blood sweat and tears that any small businesses put into their craft of building up a successful business from the ground up and to not receive the correct compensation is troubling. Overall, enjoy the process because it will be worth it in the end when payday comes and if it never does that's ok, continue to run your business and make more money.

What is the key to maximizing growth and scaling while positioning your business for an exit enabling for you to get the most amount of money?

It is about knowing when to sell and having good fundamental strategies and executing those strategies. It can be the difference from make a few hundred thousand dollars to making many millions or even billions. It really is that big of a difference.

About 50% of all businesses survive at the 5-year anniversary mark. About 30% of businesses make it to 10 years. A small business (for this definition under 100 people) make up 98.2% of all businesses and employ 59 million people and make up 44% of the economy in the United States, important and significant. What other industry or thing you can do that the longer you are in it, the greater chance of failure you have.

An important aspect when getting into a business is do I create a job for myself, or do I want to build the business and create wealth? The amount of time it takes to create a job or build massive wealth is the same. The separation is the strategy and execution.

As anyone in business knows it is never easy and takes dedication, hard work and thick skin. My job is to show you how you can work, not in your business but on your business – sell or grow and sell business for more profits. How to get your money out of the business and how to get the most amount of money for your business on a sale.

Only 20% of businesses sell. With so many businesses in the United States, it is a competitive market. Not just competitive in the field of business selling products and services but competitive for you to cash out, especially getting the most out of what you have.

Most times the average business owner does not know or understand how to first sell their business and second maximize the selling price.

Most just throw it to a fast-talking business broker that wants to lock you into a contract whether they perform or not. Regardless of the business, the numbers don't work in your favor because 80% of all businesses never sell. The broker will lock you into a contract put it on a website and just by pure volume and almost no work, they sell a few companies and yes, you guessed it they sold for less than what the hard-working owner should have received but they still get their commission.

But there is a formula to maximize the sale price.

First, you must know what how much money you need out of the business on a sale and what your expectations - financially are and what do you need once you exit. If your business is worth $3 million dollars and you need $10 million dollars to maintain your lifestyle to have the fun and enjoyment, you deserve.

Then you have a wealth gap. The difference between the $3 million current price and the $10 price you need is $7 million.

Second, if your business has a net income of $300,000. The income is usually calculated by the average income for the last 3 years, you multiply this by the standard industry selling multiple, which are industry standards, but not all businesses are equal. Let's say the multiple is 4 for your business which would make the business worth approximately $1.2 million.

Something to keep in mind and many people do not understand or know is that the multiples for a business sale have a range – from a low-end business to a high-end business, meaning that if the procedures and infrastructure are not good it would be classified as a low-end business. If the company can implement strategies and execute the company could graduate all the way up to a "best in class" business where that multiple could be 4 which makes that business sell for approximately $3.6 million dollars. That is 4 times the profit for the same business. This is called a profit gap.

The third area is your personal plan and where do you see yourself in 3 years, 5 years, and beyond?

It is important to take these three factors into account in the beginning and revisit often. This will help drive the next key decision.

An important aspect for a business seller is attractiveness. The attractiveness relates to what the business looks like to outside potential buyers. Does the company run without the owner, is there a concentration of the customer base, does the company have high turnover, are they bringing new products or services to the market, and many other factors are taken into consideration. The more attractive, the higher the multiple which can take that wealth gap and multiple that by millions.

Another crucial factor and probably the most important of them all is readiness. Is the owner ready to sell the company or do they want to hold on to it?

Businesses like most everything in life are either growing or dying. If the owner is not ready to sell, they should be strategically and actively growing. There are proven and assessed fundamental strategies that can multiply the bottom and top line of a business. It takes about the same amount of effort that you normally exhaust, why not use the same time, and get that much more. You can outrun Mother Nature, but you will never beat Father Time. That is why if a business owner is either stale, tired or cannot hit that next level, it is important to bring in an expert to help kick start the growth. There are strategies, examples and stories in the following chapters that can accelerate your growth.

Why is readiness important? Because most business sales that have a contract to sell fall apart because the owner is not ready to sell. Primarily the owners are still emotionally attached and do not know what is next in their life and what they are going to do but that is a personal decision. In the meantime, you can prepare to maximize your business asset while you are still driving the ship and get the most out of your greatest asset.

What makes a business attractive to a buyer? An owner that can step away and the company still run efficiently without them. These types of businesses command a higher multiple and provide the most amount of selling profits.

This book is designed to be more like a manual where you can reference ideas, thoughts, and strategies with a quick reference index in the back.

There are ways to sell a business and many strategies it is not one size fits all and in later chapters, we will dive into that.

Also, on the flip side, you can expand your business by making strategic acquisitions whether you just pick up their customers, assets, or distribution. This is a way to expand your business and make it attractive and worth more on a sale.

You can sell the business in many ways. The better systems that are in place combined with a highly polished presentation the bigger the return. There are ways that instead of you waiting for someone to knock on your door to buy your business, you can tap on theirs and they will come running with money falling out of their pockets to take your business over and to pay you. We will explore that in later chapters

I just wanted to lay a light foundation that if you only read these few pages, you can gain some valuable insight. Most books that are bought are never read. I want this one not just to be read but to be actionable.

Timing the sale right is the biggest key, but how do you know if the timing is right? The answer is you never really do know, but you can position and plan to maximize the value and the cash in your favor.

1. Prepare and build the story of the business. This is the most important part. You need to impart emotion, potential, and describe a future for the business. If you

have a company losing a million dollars a year or more and your story is strong enough, you can realize money from the company: think Tesla.

2. The story should be short and sweet and include the history, the struggles, and the change that is anticipated to double or triple the sales or the income. For example, you have a Chinese restaurant that was started four years ago, and business was exceptionally good until they built a new road and really hurt the business. Consequently, you had to reinvent how to provide service to your customers. Starting next month, you will be in full swing. You are going to advertise with Uber Eats, a college student advertising group that passes flyers out at locations driving people to call and place orders. They target different areas throughout a four-week period. You also expanded your lunch menu and set up a buffet in four new office buildings for all weekdays during the month. You are getting ready to explode with growth but unfortunately, for health reasons, you must sell the business. What a horrible time for you after all this challenging work, but the next owner will benefit. Under this scenario, the business is worth.

3. It is usually better to sell on an upswing, but sadly, most businesses never have an upswing.

MAKE SURE YOUR BOOKS ARE IN ORDER

It is important to have your books and records in order. Normally, small business owners keep their books and records as though it is their own personal account. However, when selling the company, it can be really confusing to a buyer because they don't know what is true. The small business owner's normal strategy is to minimize taxes, pay less and keep more in their pockets.

When trying to sell the company, the opposite is true. You need to maximize the amount of taxes you pay because that shows documented income. The more income you have, the greater the value of the business. There are two ways to do this. The first way is to maximize your tax position, eliminate all personal expenses, and any other business expenses that could be construed as non-business expenses, and file and pay your taxes on that income. The prospective buyer will ask for and verify the tax returns, make sure they match. The second is to leave your tax situation the same and do what is called reconciliation/add-backs from your tax return to your profit and loss statements. Suppose your tax return shows a loss of $10,000, and you can add these expenses: $30,000 for your kids' salary, $50,000 to your salary, $5,000 for car expenses, $15,000 for other personal expenses. These expenses are added back in, and your income would be $90,000. You can do this, and it is acceptable.

You also must list your expenses by line item and what they are year after year. You'll need a list of all your assets like furniture, equipment, accounts receivable, etc.

What is the most asset that a company can have? The customers and/or the distribution are the most valuable assets. If you have someone that is buying a product, that is more important than having any equipment or product. Give me a customer list, and I can find products to sell to them.

For more information or get involved with us reach out to Jan Capital Inc. www.jancapitalinc.com

COMBINE WITH A COMPANY THAT IS GOING OUT OF BUSINESS BEFORE YOU SELL

One smart operator had a plumbing supply business that he wanted to sell but his sales were flat and slowly shrinking. He found a competitor that was in a comparable situation, and they combined the customers and their inventories. Then they sold the excess property and equipment and then sold the much larger business. Each business was netting around $60k per year, and within nine months, the company was sold, and each seller pocketed over 1 million dollars. If they had sold separately, they would have been lucky to get $300k each. A win for both and both is out of a situation where all they really owned was a job.

WHAT CREATES VALUE IN A BUSINESS?

To attract a buyer, you need multiple ways that will drive income to the business. You need a good customer base, distribution, and multiple distribution channels and a well-trained customer-focused team that will enable the business to continue. If you only have one type of customer and one type of product, you should expand that before selling. As stated above, with the customer base, you could sell complementary products. You do not have to make them, and they do not have to be exclusive, but you can offer those products because it is convenient.

See the marketing section for more details on this strategy.

Buyers want to buy a business with many customers. If only a few customers make up most sales, losing one customer can be devastating. A buyer likes to see a diverse customer base with multiple selling opportunities to reduce risk. If you can lock the customers into contracts, that gives the buyer more comfort.

If the owner is the sole employee, there will not be much to sell unless it is an arbitrage internet company or a popcorn vendor. If these are the case, it is harder to get a lot of cash; the business could disappear fast, and it is a part-time job at best. You must be able to provide a transition team to give the buyer comfort.

POOL AND LOAN

One smart operator had a 3rd generation, family-owned company that made heavy equipment. They hated the business that their grandfather started, but through the years, it provided a good lifestyle for them. As the global economy was expanding, competition was creeping into the market. The competition's machines were half the price, and their market and customer base were shrinking. The parts business was more profitable than the heavy machinery segment. It was lucrative to sell parts for all the old machines in the field and the combined business still had a profit of about $100k.

The strategy they employed was threefold. First, they became the distributor for the forging unit, which was half the price. The company had an extensive customer list with relationships that spanned over 50 years or more. They captured sales that they would have lost to the competition selling the cheaper models. Second, they bought out a competitor who was doing little business but had an extensive customer list and a lot of heavy manufacturing equipment. They closed the purchase on Friday morning and had an auction sale on Saturday, which netted over $500k after paying the owner the purchase price. Third, he was increasing his bank loans. The reason for this was that he wanted to sell the company for no money down and got the bank to finance the purchase.

He found an industry sales group that assumed the bank debt and the business for no money down. The smart Operators netted $2.5 million and were out of the business they hated.

KEEP IT QUIET

Having confidentiality when selling your business is important, especially with employees because they will be afraid of being out of a job and they might not like the new owner. Selling businesses is not like selling a house. It's important to keep it under wraps until the sale is completed. You should make a concerted effort to help the new owner with the transition. If you consider one or two of your employees as valuable, you can include them late in the selling process, but also explain that the new owner needs them and give them a bonus upfront as a show of good faith. The upfront bonus doesn't have to be a large amount of cash, but the gesture will buy a lot of goodwill and loyalty.

LET THE EMPLOYEES BUY YOU OUT

One smart operator had a furniture manufacturing company that had 32 employees; many of the employees had been there for many years and the turnover was low. He wanted to retire and move to Florida; the company was moderately profitable at about $200k per year. The company had independent sales reps throughout the country. He had a general manager and a plant/manufacturing manager. The owner attempted to sell the company for two years with no luck. He got the two managers together and asked if they would like to buy the company with the other employees, and they all wanted to become an owner. The employees could scrape the money together, but the owner had a strategy. The employees combined had 401k and retirement accounts that were worth over 1.5 million dollars. The owner went to the bank and set up a loan on the assets of the company, property plant and equipment and accounts receivable for 1 million dollars. The employees took out a loan against the retirement account of 1 million dollars. The employees gave the owner 2 million dollars, and he moved to Florida. The fascinating thing with this transaction was that after the employees took over, the profits increased to $600k per year because they were more efficient and conscious of the expenses. It was a win for the owner and the employees.

HOW TO FIND A BUYER

There are two primary ways to find a buyer. One is strategic and the other is the traditional market way. The strategic way is to pick out a competitor or find a company that will complement your business. The advantage is that the cost structure changes, and it could mean a lot more profits to be made because the overhead can be reduced by combining the infrastructure, sales, and service sections of the business.

The second way is to use a traditional business broker who has access to a database of buyers searching to purchase businesses. The broker is paid when the business sells.

The reality is that the percentage of businesses listed versus those that are sold is small. If you want to use a broker, make sure you get one with a proven record of success. Do your homework on the broker. Get testimonials from satisfied business sellers and ask them how they sold their company. The fee to a broker is usually 10%.

LOSING BUSINESS SOLD FOR MAX DOLLARS

One smart operator had a printing company that made little money. The printing business is tough and has slim margins. The Operators couldn't sell the company and weren't making any real money but had a good reputation. He decided to broker his relationship with his customers to a competitor for a 15% commission. Initially, he was only making 3% per year. They went from making $30,000 a year working 60 hours a week to making $150,000 a year working 5 hours per week, and the arrangement has lasted more than five years.

IF IT DOESN'T WORK THE FIRST TIME, DO IT AGAIN AND AGAIN

One smart operator had a spray shop and was making about $60k per year. He had equipment that was worth about $150k. He sold the company through a broker for $60k down and financed the balance of the $300k at $5k per month. He sold his business three times before all was said and done. He received $180k in down payments and another $85k in monthly payments and was still owed $300k.The first two owners didn't like the business and tried to get the former owner to buy it back, but he refused but told them he'd let them out of the contract. And he sold the business again.

For more information or get involved with us reach out to Jan Capital Inc. www.jancapitalinc.com

Chapter 2

BUYING BUSINESSES

It does not have to be your idea to make money

"The best way to predict the future is to create it." – Peter Drucker, Management Consultant and Author

As We discussed before, there is not one way to buy a business. Each business offers a different value in the market and depending on where your focus is on the company and how you should think about approaching it. For instance, if you have a company that you know is profitable and you're a little interested or have family that was previously in that business there is an opportunity for you to get into that business and use your knowledge and resources to help the business scale even more. The false narrative is that one must have all the money themselves and the idea but, you don't have to go that way. You don't have to have either, but if you use an idea that has been proof of concept, then you're able to recreate in a way that fits well with the market and grow it that way you see fit best.

Once you decide you want to be an entrepreneur and decide what industry you want to be in initially. Things can always change and if you decide you want to pivot into something else, that's perfectly fine because you use the tools you learned and apply them into the next adventure. Buying a business whole or even buying a small piece of it is better than nothing. No matter what you will get the experience that is needed for you to take the next step in your career. As my mother always told me, "Son you must start somewhere "and for many years I didn't understand that concept because I was always the type to want to know it all or have it all figured out before I start. As I got older, I understood more that the concept my mom was teaching me was that whether you have the whole pie or sharing it with others, at least you're a part of something.

Buying into a business doesn't always mean cash, sometimes it's your relationships, your time and energy that you put into the company could be more than enough to get you a piece of equity. For better terms, I call it a "piece of a pie" because it helps me better visualize that I have a small piece of bigger because once it's sold as a whole, my piece will be worth much more. I can tell you many ways that you can buy, create, or sell a business and they all have the same elements, one just must understand the value of the company at each stage.

I remember starting my first company called "Tough Choices" which is a brand that supports giving back to youth to help the next generation. This was in 2019, fast forward 3 years later and I've learned so much about partnering, selling a piece of your business to be a part of another company that could help everyone involved grow. If there is one thing I can tell you, there is no right or wrong way to buy a business. The most important thing is understanding what it is that you want and how to accomplish it with the company that you're buying into.   Once you have a plan on how you want to purchase and how you will turn it into more. Success is right around the corner for us all, it's about finding the correct fit for your wants and needs and once it all clicks, you will be officially breaking through the barriers.

The Landlord's game invented by Elizabeth Magie was the precursor of the game Monopoly. She patented the game in 1904. The game was handwritten and was shared among neighbors, and marketing was done by word of mouth. Ruth Hoskins used Atlantic City names and added them to the game boards. Charles Darrow learned the game from his wife and created the game Monopoly and had it printed. His version had a more professional presentation. He obtained the copyright to the game in 1933 and began a large-scale distribution through stores. Then he took the next step – sell the product line. He approached Milton Bradley Company, which owned Battleship, The Game of Life, Twister, Yahtzee, and others. Milton Bradley rejected Darrow's presentation. Parker Brothers heard about the game and the sales growth and approached Darrow and bought him out. At this time, there were over 15 different variations of games like

Monopoly that were homemade and being sold or just duplicated among neighbors. Darrow saw the opportunity, repackaged it, copyrighted the version with slight variations and profited.

MAKE YOUR PASSION YOUR BUSINESS

One smart Operator loved to race his car. He started at the age of 16. Racing is an expensive hobby, but he loved it more than anything. When he turned 18, he had a choice to go to college or get a job. He found someone who had a used parts business but wanted to sell because he wasn't making money. He had an inventory of used parts worth $30,000 but was terrible at sales. The smart Operators went to him and asked if he could sell the parts and pay him after they were sold, and of course, the guy said yes. At the next racing event, he listed the parts and passed out flyers and within a week, he sold $50k worth of parts. He paid the original owner $10k for all the parts and reinvested the $40k to buy more inventory. He built a business that now makes over $100k per year. But more importantly, he gets to race for free because the car and the events are advertising for him.

WHAT IS BETTER: START A BUSINESS FROM SCRATCH OR PURCHASE AN EXISTING?

All small businesspeople know that there are diverse ways to be in business. The two primary options are: starting a new business or buying an established one. Often, people are confused as to which option is best. Each opportunity has its own advantages and disadvantages. However, buying an existing business allows you to have cash flow immediately.

STARTING A BUSINESS

Starting a new business from scratch can be rewarding, and usually, it revolves around a unique product, idea, technology, or marketing plan. One of the advantages of this option is that you can start small with minimal upfront cash and expand the sales and capacity down the road. Another advantage is that you can evaluate your business idea from limited space and with minimal risk.

Starting a successful business requires more than just getting a business idea and taking it to market. It involves understanding the market, the product, who the customers are, and the potential profit combined with other factors. Many times, the individual falls in love with the idea itself and doesn't really factor in the risk and odds of success; initially, the idea makes sense, but they fail to follow through and understand the risks. In the real world, there may be little or no demand for that business, product or idea, or the competition may be so tough that starting the business would mean fighting an impossible battle.

Starting a new business has a lot of risks and many disadvantages. You must attract customers who do not know who you are, and the startup usually requires a lot of time, money, and effort. You may have to support the business with your own money because there may be little or no profits for the first few months or perhaps years; ouch! Also, obtaining startup funding is exceedingly difficult because few want to invest in a high-risk startup that will most likely fail; most startups fail early.

BUYING A BUSINESS

This can be a more effective, efficient, and cash-flow positive way to own a business. However, this method is usually much more expensive than a startup. The owner of an existing business normally will expect you to pay for all the effort, time, money, and goodwill that he put into making the business. Also, he built a base of customers, established the cash flow and brand, worked to be ahead of the competition, hired and trained employees, and overcame market challenges.

An existing business purchase has many advantages; the biggest advantage is the cash flow on day one. Banks will loan you the needed financing to acquire an existing business because it has an established history and assets. The risks associated with buying an existing business are smaller because the business has trained employees, an existing customer base, operating processes, a known location, and an existing cash flow.

However, buying a business comes with some disadvantages; one of which is the contingent liabilities associated with buying a new business. You can protect yourself from these liabilities by structuring the transaction as an asset purchase.

Let's compare starting a new business with buying an existing one based on certain criteria, such as risk factors, rewards, management challenges, and so on.

RISK FACTORS OF BUYING VS. STARTING YOUR OWN BUSINESS

Starting a business usually involves high risks and most startups fail. The startup cost is a crucial factor. For example, if you start up a powder coating shop, you could spend $200k for the equipment and another $100k on becoming established in the market and building a customer base. Whereas, when buying a business, the equipment has been amortized, meaning it is used and worthless, and your upfront cost could be much less than a startup and it has immediate cash flow from existing customers. Start-up business owners must deal with many unknowns, such as whether customers will buy the products and services, and whether the business will be profitable in the long term. On the other hand, an existing business has a reputation in the market and loyal customers. The challenge lies in building upon what has been accomplished.

WHO ARE YOU BUYING FROM?

There are two types of sellers: one seller is the actual owner, and it is personal to them. They started the business; they built the business, and it is their baby. Unless you want to overpay to this seller, you must strategize and use a technique that makes them like you. They want to sell to someone who is going to ensure that their "baby" will survive, and they will be paid. You must develop rapport and get them to like you. Listen to their story of how they made the company and find the hot button as to why they want to sell. Most often, it is not just about the money, it's about the future of the business and the possibility that they will be paid. Once you can determine what the hot button is, you can structure a deal. After that, test the deal structure on the phone or in person, and get buy-in and then write a letter of understanding that will be binding.

1. Let them talk and tell their story.

2. Why are they selling?

3. What is their hot button? If someone is sick in the family, they are too tired to work, they want to spend more time with the family or many other reasons. Once you know what is driving them to sell, it will give you the information to effectively structure the deal to fit their hot button.

4. Pre-frame with a soft punch. Once all the positives have been discussed, start explaining the negatives to bring down the value of the business but don't do this with arrogance – always be respectful.

5. Evaluate a deal concept in person or over the phone. Explain your rough concept, such as, "I was thinking of $50k down and $2k a month for 2 years and I know you want to take a vacation. I'll pay for you and your family to go to Hawaii."

6. Write a letter of understanding.

7. Draw up a contract, if necessary. Many businesses have been sold on a two- or three-page letter of understanding.

BUYING FROM A LARGE CORPORATION

If you're buying a company from a large corporation, there could be many great deals with this scenario. It is not personal to the seller, and it is all about the numbers. Sometimes the business could be failing and causing more problems than it is worth, and they just want to get rid of it. The inside strategy is that the selling price could be just a little higher than the net book value of the assets. This means that they normally don't account for reasonable value or market presence but strictly want to unload from a book value standpoint. This can create a fantastic opportunity for a buyer. The difficulty is that a lot of times this is not advertised but known only by word of mouth or by an insider.

VALUATION ISSUES WHEN BUYING A BUSINESS

Every good decision you make with a startup creates value in the business. However, when you are buying an existing business, you are paying for the already created value. How much you are willing to pay for the business depends on your evaluation of the company's potential as well as its history.

HIDDEN PROBLEMS OF BUYING A BUSINESS

Certain market realities may be hidden from a prospective buyer. Even due diligence may fail to reveal certain difficulties that an existing business is facing, such as new competitors coming into the market. If experienced professionals participate in the due diligence process, most of these potential problems will be detected, but not always. Make sure a representation and warranties clause are included in the contract.

MANAGEMENT CHALLENGES OF BUYING A BUSINESS

When you are starting a new business, you will be responsible for hiring the best individuals to join your team. When you buy a business, you inherit the people already in place, and it takes time to get rid of the poor performers. Employees may not like the new owner, and the old employees may have resistance to change since there are existing policies, procedures, and an established corporate culture.

REWARDS OF BUYING

Start-up companies usually go through a painful period during which they must spend money without earning any and waiting for the cash can put you out of business quickly. Even if there is positive cash flow, normally these funds are reinvested into marketing and other business costs. It can take time for the business to start making a profit. When you buy a business, the financial rewards could begin as soon as the transaction closes. It depends on how the business was purchased: cash up front, financed over time or a combination. Cash flow could be tight depending on the structure of the deal you made, and the debt load you take on and the payment amounts for the loan.

The advantages of buying an existing business outweigh the challenges. Paying the extra costs for an established business is better than facing the risks of starting a new business from scratch.

With the aging of the baby boomer generation, many more companies are being sold and listed for sale. The ones that are highly profitable and running like a well-oiled machine usually have an extremely high purchase price and are much harder to buy. The sweet spot is the business in the lower category. It may be losing money or just squeaking by. Often the reason is obvious, and it allows for a fantastic opportunity to quickly turn it around while paying a lower price. Some reasons these businesses do not do well are poor management practices, lack of financing, lack of cash flow, tough competition, and many other reasons. These problems create opportunities for buyers. Many small business owners make a tough decision to sell, and buyers take advantage of these distressed businesses and pay low prices.

An effective way to get into a new market instead of a startup is to locate and purchase a distressed business that is operating in the market you want to enter. You could also double your business by combining their losing business with yours and obtain their sales with none of the overhead; this is called business pooling.

Buying a distressed or low-profit business takes savvy individuals to find but they are out there. The process is more than just scouring the Internet for businesses. Finding, evaluating, and buying a distressed business can take a long time and there are many inherent risks and problems that are not involved in buying a strong company.

BUY A BUSINESS IN DEBT OR IS LOSING MONEY

1. Preparing for the acquisition

One of the first things to do when purchasing a distressed business is to make sure you are adequately prepared. Define the goals and objectives and specify the criteria you are looking for in prospective target companies. Are you looking to pool a business, looking to buy a stand-alone and cut costs or are looking to liquidate the assets and close the business down? You need to determine what you want, why you want it, and how it fits into your overall objectives; you need to create a detailed plan.

The objectives should be clear, articulated, and well-documented. You need to determine the size of the transaction, funds required to purchase the business and maintain operations, the type of business, the profit potential, and many other considerations. They should be put in writing and ranked based on priority. Many buyers want to purchase a distressed business, but they don't use common sense or determine their objectives before rushing to complete the purchase. This will occur when the target business is being offered at a low price and they are nervous about missing the opportunity.

Not determining the goals and objectives upfront is a big mistake. If the objectives upfront are quantified and the business doesn't meet them, there is a good chance it will underperform in both the short and long term and buying is a huge mistake. Straying from the objectives and the purchase criteria is one of the worst decisions a business owner makes and difficult to recover from.

2. Perform due diligence

Purchasing a distressed business or any business can tempt the buyer into skipping due diligence; not doing effective due diligence could be fatal and not only kill that business but could also kill any business the owners have and hurt them personally. Doing proper and effective due diligence and knowing exactly what you are buying is important to detect issues and potential pitfalls. Due diligence can prevent the unexpected or foreseeable problems that may jump up and bite you later.

In addition to the financial records, every aspect of the business must be reviewed and understood; this includes operations, management, equipment and assets, suppliers, customer relationships, and employees. If your prospective purchase is a manufacturer, you need to understand and review its relationships with vendors. This will determine whether you will be able to take advantage of existing relationships, possibly establish added terms with current suppliers, or even find new suppliers.

Since the customers are the most important ingredient of any business, it is important to evaluate those relationships. This normally will create challenges because most distressed businesses have tense relationships with customers because of inventory shortages and/or negative perception. Understand the reason behind the tense relationships and determine whether they can be salvaged when you take over.

Analyze the employees as they are the strength of the business and the path to operating profitability. Usually, when a business is in trouble, morale can be exceptionally low. Furthermore, employees in these companies have not received pay raises and usually have been given more responsibility because of layoffs and staff shortages. A purchaser needs to understand the employees' situation and have a plan to manage the issues.

3. Complete the acquisition

Once you complete the due diligence of acquisition, funds can be transferred. Be sure your paperwork for the purchase agreement is tight and once you sign the legal documents, and the payment is complete, the transfer of ownership will be immediate.

INSIDE SECRETS FOR BUSINESS BUYING

Buying an established business is a fast way to get into a market. You can bypass many of the difficulties, challenges, and hassles that are inherent with a startup. The big advantage is that the company is generating cash on day one and has goodwill with the customers.

To make sure your purchase turns out to be positive and successful instead of frustrating and disappointing, you must plan and set concrete objectives with timelines, think things through and manage all aspects as many unanticipated problems and issues will certainly surface.

1. Why does the seller want to divest?

Usually, there is a good reason a small business owner wants to sell a business it took them years to build. The reason could be a red flag. Before negotiating the purchase, ask the seller why he wants to sell the business. The reason could be bankruptcy, loss of interest in running the company, income losses, tough competition, or retirement. Knowing the seller's reason can assist you in making a good decision about whether to purchase the company.

2. Due diligence

Many small business owners get caught up in the excitement of something new and they lose track of common sense. They rush into the purchase process without understanding and studying the business. It is important to understand all aspects of the business you want to purchase before completing the deal. This will enable you to see both sides of the business - good and bad. Don't get caught up in the emotions; a bad deal is still a bad deal, and it could be detrimental to your business success.

3. Don't buy an 'obscure' business

Most sellers will provide documents that show the details and records of the business, but do not rely on these alone. Visit the business to understand how it operates both from an investor's point of view and that of a customer. Examine and observe the equipment during normal operation, watch the staff, and compare what you see to what the seller has shown and told you. If you sense any discrepancies, be careful.

4. Don't invest in what you don't understand

If you don't know or understand the type of business you intend to purchase, the amount of due diligence you perform can't help you make the right decision. After purchasing the business, you will be inexperienced, and the risk is increased immensely. Even if you have no intention of managing the business yourself, you must have a fundamental concept of the business and its principles to succeed or you'll need to rely on others with experience to give you guidance.

5. Have a top price in mind from the outset

A common mistake when buying a new business is overextending financially. When the debt is so great, it is hard to survive because you will almost always have to increase the profits and the sales from day one, which puts you at a disadvantage. You must set aside some extra cash reserves for the maintenance and the well-being of the business after the acquisition.

6. Understand the importance of the owner

A lot of business owners are irreplaceable and they, essentially, are the business. If the seller is working all the time and is the main go-to guy, you need to be cautious. Are there reasons for this? Maybe the employees are not trustworthy, or the owner is a workaholic. Do they have good relationships with the customers? You need to understand the role of the owner. Additionally, you need to determine who has relationships with the customers. This is a key component because if the sales manager has good relationships with the customers, they could leave and take the customers with them and leave you holding the bag. One Operator got slammed this way; he bought a company from the owner and did not realize that the sales manager had relationships with the customers. Since the Operator was a salesperson, he fired the other sales manager. The fired sales manager went to a competitor and took 60% of the business with him within two months, ouch!

7. Ask the seller to stay on board for a time

Buying a new company is not like buying a boat. In most situations, a buyer will need the seller to stay with the company for a while to transfer the experience, trivial details, and knowledge. If a seller is reluctant to help during the transition, that's another red flag. They might be hiding something.

8. Ask for seller financing

Even though you may have enough money to purchase the business, always get the seller to finance some of the purchase price. This will give him an incentive to transfer his knowledge because if they have the rest of their money, they need to help you succeed. If you are getting seller financing because you want to structure the payment terms of the acquisition, two things happen; first, you will get better payment terms from the seller than you would from a bank or other financial institution, and second, they are vested in your success.

9. Buy with the future in the mind

Due diligence includes the books and records of the business but also a perception of the future. Will the products or services that the business currently sells be obsolete or irrelevant in the future? Are there regulatory issues that could affect the business? What is the competitive landscape? What are the trends in the industry and how fast do they change? Are they selling a protected product, patented, or do they sell a commodity? Is the market driven by price, service or quality and is the market expanding or dying?

LEGAL ISSUES WHEN BUYING A BUSINESS

Full Disclosure: The seller must agree to make full disclosure of all issues regarding the business. It is illegal for a seller to fail to disclose information to the buyer or to give false or misleading information. As a buyer, you can seek redress under the law if a seller has misled you or disclosed false information in the process of selling the business to you. Before the negotiation stage, ensure that the seller signs a disclosure document promising to supply all necessary information that is true and correct and this will assist you, the buyer, in making informed decisions.

Ownership Structure of the Business: Another issue that must be determined is the ownership structure. The business can either be bought as a sole proprietor, a trust, a company, or a partnership. You should consider these issues for asset transfers, personal protection, and tax effects.

Non-Disclosure Agreement: Before negotiating a purchase, have both parties sign a non-disclosure agreement. This is different from the full disclosure agreement discussed above. Non-disclosure is designed to protect both buyer and seller from the release of sensitive information that may have a negative effect on either party.

Right to sell: Another issue to consider is whether the person selling the business has the right to sell the business. What's the ownership structure of the business? Are there are partners and if there are other owners, do they all agree to sell? You also need to determine the shareholders' structure, and if any issues of bankruptcy or insolvency exist. It is important to obtain written statements and guarantees to this effect.

The value of the business: You need to determine the value of the business before you can make an offer. You also need to know if the company is properly registered with the necessary regulatory agencies and if there are any existing non-compliance or legal issues. The business assets, such as equipment and machinery are important too; a complete list of assets must be provided as well as a list of exclusions. The value of the assets must also be determined, and all assets must be inspected to ensure that they are in good working condition. Other assets like inventory, intellectual property, debtors, creditors, and cash must also be reviewed.

Mortgages, Encumbrances, and Charges: It is the seller's duty to resolve all issues of outstanding mortgage payments. All encumbrances on assets, inventory, and equipment must also be settled by the seller. In some circumstances, if the buyer desires a reduced purchase price, the seller can transfer the liability. The advantage to the buyer is that it can reduce the purchase price and the owner's personal liability by doing this. They can shift the company debt to the new company and pay a lot less, and a smaller down payment, for the acquisition.

Knowledge of the industry: Every industry has its rules, regulations and governing bodies. Food and drug production companies, for instance, must adhere to FDA rules. It is important for the buyer to understand these rules completely so they know exactly what they will be facing and how to comply with regulations and reporting.

Business Restrictions: You must also address issues of restrictions. You may need to have the seller sign a non-competing agreement to restrict him from trading in this type of business.

Employee Related Issues: It is also up to you as the buyer to determine whether to retain the current employees. This is important because sometimes a company's success depends on its existing staff. You must be careful about deciding whether to retain or terminate certain employees.

Payment/Funding: There should also be a solid agreement as to how the payments will be made. If there is seller financing or installment payments, the agreement must be detailed and signed.

DUE DILIGENCE CHECKLIST

1. Financial information: Analyze the purchase by checking the financial information and records for the past five to seven years.

- Income statements, balance sheets, cash flows, and footnotes.

- Review the budget versus actual expenses and management financial reports.

- Determine the breakdown of sales, gross profits, and gross profit by product type, profits by channels, and profits by region.

- Determine the current order backlog of customer sales.

- Accounts receivable aging schedule.

- Review all assets and physically inspect and compare them to the asset list.

- Review the accounts payable and match them against the payments.

- Call the customers, verify some of the orders and ask what their normal purchase cycle is and compare that to the company's records.

- Interview key employees: this will give you great insight

- Contact some employees who recently left the company and ask them why they left.

FINANCIAL PROJECTIONS

Understand and review quarterly financial projections for the next three fiscal years.

- Review the revenue by product type, customer, and channel.

- Review income statements, balance sheets, and cash.

- Understand the company's growth drivers and determine if they are effective in realizing projections.

- Review the predictability. The more predictable, the more accurate the projections are.

- Understand projected capital expenditures, depreciation, and working capital.

- Determine any plans for external financing.

- Know the industry and pricing to see if sales and profit figures are obtainable.

- Check risk factors like exchange rate fluctuation and government instability.

CAPITAL STRUCTURE

If the company is a sole proprietorship or partnership, there's not much to do. But if it is a corporation, you will need to do the following:

- Review the list of all stockholders with shares, options, warrants, or notes.

- Review all outstanding current shares.

- Review the summary of all debt instruments or bank lines with key terms and conditions.

- Review off-balance sheet liabilities.

OTHER FINANCIAL INFORMATION

You will also need to review the current federal, state, and foreign taxes, the company's general accounting policies and the schedule of financial history for equity, warrants, and debt.

BUSINESS INFORMATION

Products or services: After reviewing the business's financial information, analyze the products or services that are sold, do a breakdown of customers, applications, historical and current growth rates, market share, cost structure, profitability, the timing of new products, product enhancements, and speed and nature of technological changes.

Customer and supplier information: Customers and suppliers are the main ingredients of a successful business. It is necessary to investigate them when considering buying a company. During the due diligence process, request for the following:

- List of top 15 customers for the past two or three years with full contact and purchase details of each and current year-to-date purchases.

- List of strategic relationships.

- Details of revenue by each major customer.

- Descriptions of any significant relationships discontinued within the last two to three years.

- List of top 10 suppliers for the past two to three fiscal years with full contact and supply details of each.

Competition: The success of a business in any sector hinges largely on the competition. You need to analyze the company's competition. Determine the company's market position with respect to strengths and weaknesses within the marketplace. Analyze and understand the basis of the competition, i.e., price, technology, service, distribution, etc.

Marketing, Sales, and Distribution: Analyze the marketing programs and strategies along with the opportunities and risks. Review the position of the company in the market, its products, and its domestic and international distribution channels. Know the major customers in terms of status and trends as well as prospects for future growth and development; the avenues for generating new business; the ability and strength to implement the marketing plan with current and projected budgets; and a sales force productivity model for compensation, quota average, sales cycle, and plan for new hires.

Research and development: Understand the company's strategies for research and development, key personnel, and major activities. Analyze the new product pipeline based on the cost of development, required technology, risks, status, and timing.

Management and personnel: Understand the organizational chart and the historical and projected headcount by function and location. Check the biographies of management and their employment history, age, service with the company, and years in their current position. Understand compensation arrangements and turnover and review any significant employee problems, past or present.

Legal and related matters: Know if there are pending lawsuits against the company or any that have been initiated by the company. You need to review environmental and employee safety issues, as well as current liabilities. Review the list of patents, copyrights, licenses, and trademarks and check any other legal documents available.

The process of purchasing a business can be very cumbersome and even professionals can become confused. There are just so many things to be done, so many factors to consider, and so many precautions to take to avoid running into problems later.

There are two major ways to manage a business purchase; you may either buy the business assets or opt for stock purchase instead.

ASSET PURCHASE

Asset purchase means that you buy the physical and non-physical assets owned by the business; the entire business as a going concern becomes yours. What makes a business after all are the assets that are combined and used to generate income. The assets that you must buy include physical assets like motor vehicles, buildings, office equipment, furniture and fittings, inventory, computers, and other assets. You could also purchase intangible assets like the company's website, its logo, existing customers and suppliers, websites, patents, trademarks, and other such intangible assets.

With an asset purchase, you can choose to retain all the current employees of the business and take over all lease rights and ownership of assets, such as lands and buildings. If the company you intend to buy has some rights it currently uses which you think would be beneficial for the going forward, you can decide to purchase those rights. For instance, such things as permits, licenses, and contracts can be transferred to you.

However, you cannot think about the assets alone. During this type of business negotiation, the liabilities of the business could also be acquired. Fortunately, you could have an agreement with the seller that allows you to choose which liabilities and assets you are willing to purchase and which ones you would rather not buy.

STOCK PURCHASE

Stock purchase, on the other hand, is a different ball game. All you must do is purchase the stocks (shares) of the business that the owner transfers to you and not just the assets. When you want to invest some of your own money, you can ask your stockbroker to help you purchase stocks; what you are doing is buying a small part of the business. You become one of the owners and the business owns all the assets. You are not just buying the chairs and the computers; you are buying ownership of the business. The extent of your ownership will depend on the percentage of shares that you own, and the profits/dividends paid to you would also be according to the percentage of the shares you own. There is no need for re-negotiations, transfer of titles, reapplications and all the other technicalities.

WHICH IS BETTER: ASSET OR STOCK PURCHASE?

Now, to the crux of the matter: which is better for you? Which offers you more benefits and protection as a buyer in a business sale negotiation? Let's consider some of the crucial factors that need to be taken into consideration.

Buying Company Stock vs. Asset Purchase: Which is the best?

a. Taxes: You should always know the tax implication of every decision you make. Taxes could impact your earnings and cash flow. If you are looking for the business purchase method that will offer the lowest tax liabilities, then you should consider buying assets versus a stock purchase. Business sellers try to avoid this type of sale because it attracts higher taxes for them, and they would prefer stock sales. However, as a buyer, asset purchase is better for you taxwise.

b. Liabilities: Asset purchase is also more favorable for a buyer when liabilities are considered. Purchasing stock of a business means that you must accept the liabilities as well. Some of these liabilities may be unknown or unwanted, but you still must accept them when you agree to a stock purchase. If you must purchase the stock, ensure that you do your due diligence and find out about the businesses' existing liabilities. If there are liabilities that you do not wish to assume, you can negotiate with the seller so that such liabilities are retained by the seller.

c. Goodwill: If you choose to purchase assets instead of stocks, you have the advantage of amortizing goodwill for tax purposes for fifteen years.

d. Complications of Procedure: Another factor to consider is the ease of each process. While stock purchases are less complicated, asset purchases are complicated because there's a lot of negotiations involved and even when the sales contract is completed, a lot of steps still must be taken by the buyer. For instance, if the company had an existing lease, the buyer may have to renegotiate the lease contract. Stock purchase, on the other hand, is easier, especially when the company has only a few shareholders.

Buying an established business can be a smart way for individuals to break into a new market without having to face the struggles of starting a new business. For corporations, it provides an avenue to expand capacity, workforce, and market share, or move into new markets. When implemented properly, this strategy can be fulfilling and financially rewarding. However, this strategy usually carries tax implications for the buyer, which range from employment taxes to state tax liabilities.

Although the tax implications of business acquisitions vary from business to business, some tax liabilities would apply in all cases. You need to understand these tax implications to help you make well-informed decisions about business acquisitions.

THE TAX IMPLICATIONS OF BUYING A BUSINESS

When you buy a business, you don't have to pay federal tax on your purchase. The seller or owner of the business must continue to pay any tax debts to the Internal Revenue Service (IRS) unless there's a tax lien, which is transferable to the new owner. However, you will most likely be responsible for other local and state tax liabilities, which vary depending on the structure of the business. If your business is unincorporated, your tax liabilities will be less because buyers normally acquire only tangible assets that have quantifiable tax obligations, such as equipment.

But if your business is a corporation, the corporate stock can place huge tax liabilities on you because most stock acquisitions free the seller of all current and future tax obligations (unless otherwise stated in the sales contract).

Local and state tax liabilities: Before, if the seller owed taxes to state and local agencies, he was still liable for the taxes even after the sale. But the rule has changed because government entities have become cash-strapped and are devising various methods to capture tax liabilities without delay. The government entities now turn to business buyers during the escrow process and request payment of the taxes due on their purchased businesses. In fact, in some U.S. states, you cannot conduct business after buying a new company until you have paid all outstanding local and state tax debts due. However, you do not have to bear this burden. Before completing the purchase, you can request that the seller settle all tax debts due and provide certified letters from tax agencies as proof of payment.

Taxes on tangible assets: If you are buying tangible assets, such as machinery and equipment, you or the seller may be required to pay local and state sales and use tax liabilities. How the assets are valued determines who will bear the greater part of the burden. Provided the assets have a high value, your tax burden will be reduced because you can apply a large tax deduction on the asset's depreciation. However, most sellers will attempt to reduce the value of their hard assets to reduce tax liabilities on any assets sold for more than their depreciated cash value. You must negotiate a fair price for the tangible assets to reduce the tax implications for both parties.

Employment taxes: The law regarding employment tax varies by state. Typically, the burden of employment taxes lies with the business owner. You can take advantage of employment tax deductions if the seller remains temporarily as a paid employee to provide training. In this case, a smart way to reduce your tax liability on the total acquisition would be to negotiate a lower selling price and pay the seller a higher wage during the training period.

GET THE MONEY TO BUY THE BUSINESS

Buying a business is an involved process and securing financing can be difficult. If you prepare, and the business is legit you can get financing.

ROLLOVER FOR BUSINESS STARTUPS (ROBS)

A Rollover for Business Startups (ROBS) is a little-known way to secure financing for a business purchase. This allows you to tap into a retirement savings account (from a 401k or IRA) without any early withdrawal taxes or penalties. It is possible to use this money to fund the down payment for an SBA. If used with the SBA, you can finance 100% of your purchase.

SBA LOANS FOR BUYING A BUSINESS

SBA loans are a suitable place to start when searching for business acquisition financing. SBA loans have competitive rates along with the best and most generous terms. The lenders can be difficult to work with because there are so many hoops to jump through due to the government guarantee.

It is much simpler to use SBA money for an existing operating business in comparison to startup financing because it is easier to gauge the cash flow and the stability of the operation. The operating business has a track record that can be analyzed, measured, and projected.

An SBA Loan is safer for the bank because the government will guarantee a substantial portion of the debt. This is a better solution because if the borrower does not have enough collateral to cover the loan a bank will have a much higher rate of interest.

LOAN AMOUNTS

With an SBA 7a loan, you can borrow up to $5 million for the purchase of a business. The lender won't fund the entire purchase price, however, so you'll need to put up a down payment equal to between 10-20% of the purchase price.

INTEREST RATES

SBA loan rates vary based on the current U.S. prime rate, which is normally around 6-9%.

FEES

SBA loans have a guarantee fee starting at 3% of the loan amount for loans over $150K. There are usually other fees charged on a loan, such as closing costs fee, application fees, and early payment fees.

REPAYMENT SCHEDULE

SBA loan payment terms vary depending on the assets and operation of the business. The maximum term for an SBA is ten years for working capital and 25 years for real estate. The longer repayment term yields lower payments, which increases cash flow, but means you pay more interest over the life of the loan. This will increase the cost of capital if you pay for the entire term, as opposed to a shorter amortization.

QUALIFY FOR AN SBA LOAN

The bank and SBA look at a ton of information to decide whether to issue a loan or not. Five primary requirements determine approval. The minimum qualifications for an SBA loan usually start with a 680+ personal credit score, a profitable business, and a 20% down payment.

PERSONAL CREDIT SCORE

If your credit score is lower than 680, getting an SBA loan will be difficult.

DOWN PAYMENT

For the SBA, you will need cash or don't bother. Most banks want you to have a down payment of 10-20% and some require as much as 30% down. You can use a ROBS if you have $50k in a retirement account.

COLLATERAL

Just because the business is profitable and you are getting a great deal, you will still need to put up some collateral. There is always a chance the business could fail, and the bank requires security. Real estate is the best collateral because it is the safest and apt to retain its value. You can use accounts receivable, equipment, vehicles, and other assets as collateral. Banks will discount the value of the assets because the value can decrease over time, and the costs of liquidating can be expensive. For example, if you have property worth $350,000, the bank might discount its value to 80%. This would give you $280K of collateral for your loan. Vehicles, equipment, and assets that don't hold their value are discounted heavier.

INDUSTRY EXPERIENCE

Banks expect 3-5 years of industry knowledge and experience. If you lack the experience, then hire a management team that has it.

FINANCIALLY STRONG BUSINESS

Lenders are typically more inclined to lend money to someone buying an existing business over someone launching their own startup because the business has a history that can be used to assess the likelihood of loan repayment. Banks want a business to have been operating for 2-5 years profitably, with stable or growing revenues. If the business has declining revenues or is not profitable, your chances of approval will be slim to none.

APPLYING SBA

Below are the main documents you'll need to submit for an SBA loan:

Purchase Agreement

The purchase agreement is the document that states:

- The final purchase price of the business
- What is being bought (stock or asset sale)
- What is required by the seller and buyer at closing
- The effective date that ownership of the business is transferred
- If the seller will help with the transition (and terms)
- Responsibility for existing liabilities

Financial Documents for the Business

To paint a picture of the company:

- Business tax returns for the last three years
- Year-to-date profit and loss statements, balance sheets, and cash flow statements
- Information on outstanding business debts
- Information on any long-term contracts
- A complete list of business assets (including year, make, model, mileage/hours)

- Rent rolls if the business has tenants

- Business leases

- Organizational documents for the business (e.g., incorporation docs and business licenses)

- Business Plan

ROLLOVER FOR BUSINESS (ROBS)

Reiterated description: ROBS helps you access your retirement savings for a business acquisition without paying any taxes or early withdrawal fees. The money is generally available in 2-3 weeks. That's a lot faster than a bank loan and especially an SBA loan. A ROBS is not a debt or loan and no payments need to be made. However, this is your retirement money so be careful how you spend it. If it makes sense and you can generate a return, it is not a bad strategy. There are a number of requirements for the ROBS during the setup phase and after to fund the business.

SELLER FINANCING

Seller financing simply means the seller agrees to finance part or all the acquisition costs. This can help buyers who have lower credit scores. It shows that the seller has confidence that the business will survive because the owner is willing to take a chance on your success and that they are assured they will get paid. Normally, the seller will finance about 15-60% of the price. The interest rates on this money are normally close to market rates (APR 6-10%) and are amortized. Details vary depending on the deal and the seller. The stronger the buyer looks, the more of the purchase price the seller will be willing to provide and the better the interest rate will be.

If the seller only covers a portion of the purchase price, the buyer will have to come up with the balance in cash, 401k, other funds, or an SBA loan. There are no specific qualifications that sellers require because all sellers have different expectations. In this scenario, most sellers will verify your credit score and will usually accept a credit score that is a lot lower than what is needed for an SBA loan.

HOME EQUITY LINE OF CREDIT (HELOC OR HEL)

A home equity line of credit (HELOC) and home equity loans (HEL) could be an option if you are willing to risk your home. This strategy has been used by 25% of small business owners to either purchase a business outright or partially fund it. A HELOC and HEL are almost the same except for how you receive the cash. A HELOC is a credit line much like a credit card and allows you to draw against the line until you hit the limit and then you only pay the interest and not the principle. A HEL is a one-time loan, and you get all the funds as a lump sum in the beginning and make monthly payments of interest and principal.

To use either a HELOC or HEL, you will need to have 20-30% equity in your home and a 620-credit score. These types of loans are usually less expensive when compared to banks or SBA loans. This financing is flexible; you can use this money for anything.

BUY WITH FRIENDS AND FAMILY

Almost 24% of all startups start with a loan from family members or friends. If you borrow money from friends and family, it is important to keep it as a business transaction. The loan should be in writing, and you should make payments as if it were a loan from a bank.

BUSINESSES BANKS DO NOT PREFER

Banks do not like high-risk or limited margin businesses. Some include:

- Grocery Stores

- Vice industries

- Businesses with a single customer

- Restaurants

- Complicated product-based businesses

BUY BUSINESS REAL ESTATE

If you purchase real estate with the business, it can immediately improve the business assets while increasing the purchase price. If you include real estate, an SBA 504/CDC loan may be a possibility. Normally, 504 loans are the most flexible and lowest cost options to finance real estate purchases.

BORROW WHEN YOU OWN ANOTHER BUSINESS

If you own more than 20% of an existing business, the bank will examine the financial position and strength of that business as part of a loan process. The bank will want to ensure that the other business you own is a strong company that will not take money from the business that you are purchasing. Another advantage if you are in this situation is you could combine collateral between the two businesses.

FIND THE RIGHT BUSINESS

Brokers are well-versed in buying and selling businesses. They can add insight when searching for a business, check the market, and assess the available businesses. They know what businesses sell in the area, and at what price. You can play one against the other and search for the best opportunity. The seller usually pays the broker. The broker gets paid on the sale and often the down payment is used to determine their commission. That is one reason to not use a broker but finding a business can be difficult.

PREPARATION

Prepare before approaching an owner, make sure your credit rating is as high as possible. Having a good credit score shows the business owner you are financially stable and responsible with assets and money. Create a resume that shows your experience and expertise in that industry and business. If your goal is to buy a restaurant and you have never operated a restaurant, it could be difficult to prove to the owner you can survive and pay him.

FIND A MOTIVATED SELLER

Research and patience are important parts of locating a business. Find a motivated seller. This can mean locating a seller whose business has been on the market for a long time, perhaps six months to a year and has had no offers. It's possible to find someone that is close to retirement and wants to have income over several years instead of a lump sum; this is a big tax advantage as well, and the seller will receive more actual cash this way. Another possibility is a partnership where one of the partners has died or one partner wants to leave the business.

FIND AN UNDERPERFORMING BUSINESS

Find a business that is slightly profitable or even losing money. These are better for you to purchase with no money down as opposed to having to pay for a highly profitable business. You need to hire experienced management in this situation to turn the business into a profitable one.

PAY ON PERFORMANCE

Pay on performance is when the owner of a business agrees to make benchmarks for performance. When the benchmarks are achieved, the owner will get paid based on the previous agreement. Benchmark measurements can take place during a one- to five-year period and could be assessed on revenues, net income, or operating income. The final amount due is capped by the purchase price. The owner might elect to be paid on benchmarks tied to revenue, and the new owner could inflate expenses to make the net income lower. An example is a lease for a car paid for by the business or the new owner being paid a higher salary.

DIG IN DEEP AND SEARCH

The best deals are not consistently advertised. Below are four ways to find a gem:

- Broker

Business brokers function like real estate agents; they facilitate the sale of businesses. They do not get paid unless the business sells.

- Search the web

Type: "[Your area] business for sale." If you are searching for a specific business like a restaurant, salon, pet store or anything else, include that in the search. Look for companies with higher sales volume and have been for sale the longest time.

- Craigslist

Go to the "for sale" area for your town, and then scroll down to "business" and search. Keep in mind that Craigslist is like the Wild West and has a lot of flakes and scammers.

- Target CPAs and Lawyers

Tell CPA's and attorneys in your area that you are in search of a certain type of business to purchase. They have personal relationships with owners and understand their situations.

WHAT IS A UCC?

A UCC lien is a notice that an individual or company has the security of the business's assets, which means that the company pledged the assets as collateral for money that was loaned to them. When taking a loan, the lender will want security against the business assets. If you agree to the loan documents, it will give a right to the lender to file a UCC with the state in which you are located. A UCC lien shows because it is filed by the date that the loan company has the rights to the assets before anyone else. The reason for the UCC is that a company cannot borrow multiple times on the same assets.

PERSONAL GUARANTEE

Unless you're able to pay cash for the business you're buying, it's likely that you will have to sign a personal guarantee. The lender will want some security other than the company assets if you default on the loan. This makes the buyer tied to the purchase and/or loan. If your story and presentation combined with your history are strong, you can often get out of providing a personal guarantee, but it is not easy and takes good planning and execution.

NOT ENOUGH FOR DOWN PAYMENT

There are alternatives to finding cash for a business purchase.

CASH OUT YOUR IRA OR 401K

Another source of cash is your retirement savings accounts. There are large taxes and penalties if you do this, but it is possible because it is your money. You will pay a 10% penalty plus taxes on the income. If the business, you are purchasing with some of your retirement funds does not work out it could destroy your security for your future retirement.

USE A LEVERAGED BUYOUT

It is easier to buy a business with no money down than most people think and it's done every day. Can you buy every business for no money down – no, but if you are diligent, you can find one, two, three, or more. The strategy used is to leverage the assets of the business you wish to acquire. It is called a leveraged buyout; purchasing the company by pledging the business assets combined with the cash flow. This is usually unknown to most small business owners and to the larger sophisticated businesspeople. Big corporations have used leveraged buyouts for a long time. This strategy is an accepted, effective, and viable business financing strategy. In the world of a small business with little or no money, leveraged purchases effectively assist in skipping the 2 to 5 years it can take to build a strong company.

This means instead of wasting months and years painstakingly and diligently attempting to expand and grow the business with your own cash, you can acquire an existing business and immediately reap the rewards. Because of this strategy, many small business owners learn how to perform leveraged buyouts due to the potential. It is a solid way to build a successful business. For a small businessperson, the traditional way to buy a business is to save the capital needed to purchase a business and to liquidate everything you own.

The other way is to start a business from nothing and work 14-hour days and put your savings and your assets at risk and hope it works out. As the new business grows and expands, all profits are reinvested right back into the business.

When a small business owner understands and executes leveraged buyouts – not using any personal cash, credit, or assets – there is little risk. More importantly, the business can start generating income and opportunity immediately. This can be done many times and can immensely build the smart Operators' portfolio and wealth. Operating and owning a company can be the source of a great income. However, the significant difference between just breaking even and making a lot of money is the small businessperson's knowledge of today's business strategies to execute a full leveraged buyout.

COMPLETE LEVERAGED BUYOUT FOR A BUSINESS

Find a business

There are many factors and variations to consider. Do you own an operating business now? Can you find a business that can complement the one you have? The strategic opportunities and questions drive the type of business you can purchase. Do you want to change your current business? Build the criteria for the business that you seek to acquire. Research and make a list of the type of company you seek to acquire - even if they are not on the market for sale. Some of the best deals are never publicized. Contact one that interests you and asks if it could be for sale. The worst thing that can happen is you are told no.

There are many Operators who list companies for sale including online marketplaces, newspapers, brokers, and directories. Using a leveraged buyout, you do not need any cash. Find a company that interests you or that complements your existing business. For example, you love scooters and love to ride them and understand the styles and the market. Perhaps you have a friend who works for a small parts manufacturer selling scooter parts. Because he works for the company, he heard the boss grumbling about retirement.

SWING LOAN WITH A DOUBLE CLOSE

Once you find a target business that the owner wants to sell, the next step is to set up a meeting and start the process. The seller should make a compelling pitch to convince you to buy. For this example, the meeting is set through your friend, and you show up at the meeting ready to ask questions.

What are the sales per year?

What is the profit?

What is the value of the inventory?

What is the value of the equipment?

Walk around and take a tour.

Now, the money question: how much do you want?

They state a price of $300,000.

What terms are you looking for?

The seller says, "all cash."

That sounds intimidating. You would need to come up with $300,000 in cash that you don't have. Don't give up yet; you need to be a little creative.

NEGOTIATE A DEAL

The key to maximizing and closing the deal is to clearly understand what the seller wants. You must build a relationship and ask more questions that are both business and personal.

What are your plans after you sell?

What are your long-term thoughts for your company after you sell?

Do they want to kick back and retire?

More than likely, they want the business to continue and see someone responsible own it because it is personal to them. They built it through blood, sweat, and tears; it is never as easy to sell as it looks.

Let's assume the seller wants to retire and desires a steady future income. The tax savings of stretching the payments out over years means they will receive more money, possibly twice as much net income by factoring in the tax savings and improve their future lifestyle.

You must prove two things to the seller – the first is that you love the business as much as they do, and the second is that you can operate it successfully and pay them.

During negotiations, you can create a stronger bond with the seller and then offer a much smaller down payment.

Most small businesses are hard to sell and most never sell, so time works to your advantage.

Let's say that the owner wants the $300k. You offer $25k down and $275k over 60 months. At first, he balks but when no more offers come in, he will be more receptive. Make sure you explain that if you did pay him the $300k, he would only net $150k after taxes and your proposal would allow him to have almost the whole amount of cash in his pocket.

OK, he comes back to you and asks for $50k down. Now what?

GET AN ASSET BASED LOAN

Find an asset-based lender. These types of lenders are like car dealership financing. With an asset-based lender, if you don't pay, they repossess the assets. Asset-based financing is not only for individuals who want to purchase vehicles – these companies' loan on all kinds of assets including business assets. The assets they consider are the collateral – cars, trucks, machinery, equipment, accounts receivable, or land and actual hard assets that have value and could be sold at auction. When you look at a business to buy, make sure you know the true value of the assets. You want to value the assets at liquidation prices, which is the value that can be received in a fire sale. Let's say in this situation the liquidation value is $200k.

Back to our example: the asset-based lender agrees to take your $200k worth of assets as collateral and loan you up to 80% of the liquidation value, or up to $160k. The challenge is that you must own the assets before you can use them as collateral. Now what?

THE SWING LOAN

You can go to a bank and get a "swing loan." In other words, you can borrow $50,000 from the bank in the morning, pay the seller, thus transferring the title and making the business yours. Then a brief time later with the assets in the business you just bought, use the assets as collateral for the asset-based lender to provide you with

$160k.With the money from the asset-based lender immediately pay the bank $50k and have $110K left over.

Suppose the banker looks at you and says that you don't have the credit to pull it off? How do you get the bank to trust you enough to loan you the $50k? The buying term is "double escrow." Both transactions are completed at the bank, the money stays at the bank the entire time. At the same moment that they make the loan you pay the loan off and you agree to put the additional $110k in an account and this is a no-risk deal for the banker.

In one room, the seller comes in and signs the papers and transfers the ownership to the buyer. The banker says, "wait a minute, I'll get your money." The buyer goes into the next room and signs the deal with the asset-based lender and gives the check to the banker and the banker then gives the seller a $50k check. The transaction is complete, and you are the owner. Neither your credit nor your cash was used for this transaction.

This is a common strategy to buy a business with marketable assets. By planning and arranging asset-based financing in conjunction with a swing loan, you can incorporate a closing for both at the same time - double escrow. This type of deal is put together for you to win, the seller wins, and the bank wins. This was really done by one smart Operators on multiple occasions.

PURCHASING INVESTMENT REAL ESTATE

Real estate is expensive, and it usually requires a high down payment. If you are buying real-estate and you put 20% down on a piece of land, you could have to wait a long time to get back into buying or you could be in big trouble if the market changes. There is another way to avoid this pitfall.

The most successful real estate investors are the most creative, not only in structuring their deals but also in financing them. Be aggressive and proactive with your financing strategies. Below are some strategies that some smart Operators have used.

BUY INVESTMENT PROPERTY CHEAP

Construction

One smart Operators really wanted to enjoy the great outdoors and spend his weekends in the mountains. Not having cash didn't stop him. He searched for investment property for a long time and tried to negotiate seller financing. By luck, he ran across a situation for a small home located in the mountains that was owned by spouses who only used the home on the weekends. Over many years, the property fell into disrepair. The older couple did not want to sell the little house because they liked it and wanted to keep using it.

The smart Operators made a proposition to repair the house. He offered to purchase the materials and provide the labor at no cost. In return, the couple allowed the Operators to personally use the property for half the year and gave him the first right of refusal option to purchase the property at a discounted price. This was a win-win for both parties; the owners got the repairs completed at no cost and had a buyer for the future. The smart Operators didn't own the property but took control of it for half the year, rented it out and could later buy it at the discounted price.

SELLER FINANCING

Seller financing is a great option: the seller provides 100% of the financing to those buyers who cannot get a loan! In less than four years, one Operator was able to explode his investment portfolio to over 80 units by implementing this strategy. Seller financing can take a lot of time and work. You must find sellers that are motivated and willing. Also, your goal is to purchase these properties at a discounted price. A good part of seller financing is how uniquely a loan can be structured. One Operator got his seller-financed loans that were structured so that he had no payments for the first 3 months after the purchase. The cash flow benefit to him was huge. This gave him time to fix the house and rent it, all without making payments. Because the property was in a high-demand rental area, it enabled him to build the assets without a great deal of cash up front.

WHOLESALE

One Operators is a wholesaler of various properties and controls more than 200 properties. Wholesaling is a "no-money-down" buying method. It is like flipping a house; wholesaling is a quick and effective real estate investment technique and strategy, but wholesalers make no repairs or upgrades to the property. The wholesaler operates as a go-between with the seller and will market the property to buyers. The wholesaler will sign a contract with the seller and act as the go-between with the buyer. The wholesaler's function is to find a buyer before the contract expires. Executing this strategy, the Operators collect a fee. These fees are typically low. The benefit of this wholesale strategy is that most of the work can be done online and over the phone; the wholesaler can implement and execute this strategy anywhere, not just locally.

JOINT-VENTURE (EQUITY)

One smart Operator likes to use joint ventures. This joint venture is common with two parties contributing cash for the down payment and then negotiating a bank loan for the balance. Below is an example:

- Partner A: $1,000

- Partner B: $1,000

- Partner B shorter-term loan: $8,000

- Bank Loan: $60,000

Partner B will provide a short-term loan payable within one year. If the loan is not paid back by the company within the timeframe, the loan is then converted to equity, and then Partner B will own 60% of the joint venture. Under this scenario, you can own 40% of a business for only $1,000.

PRIVATE LOAN

Smart Operators will use private loans. These are low-money upfront financing tactics to purchase an investment property. Operators implemented this strategy and bought many single-family homes. The private loans are structured between a private lender and the Operators. Using this strategy, you will find their terms more flexible and accommodating and easier to negotiate to structure the terms to fit your purposes. It is common to arrange no upfront payments for a short-term private loan for one year or less.

SUMMARY

There are many ways to purchase an investment property using these low and no money down tactics. Don't presume it can't be done just because you do not have enough cash for a down payment of 20%. To start and grow a real estate business, you can and will find multiple Operators for funding.

THE BANKS "WORKOUT" PERSON

When a bank loan moves from the traditional management to "workout", the rules change. When a loan is transferred to "workout", it means the bank has serious concerns about receiving payment on the loan.

This department specializes in problem loans. Borrowers are wary of being moved to the workout department because the bank will visit and inspect the assets, among other reasons.

The workout banker's strategy and behavior are economically motivated for the institutional and personal level. The banker is not always aligned with the borrowers, and that is why it is important to understand how a workout banker works and how you can profit from it.

THE RULES CHANGE IN WORKOUT SCENARIOS

Most loans that go into a workout don't have a successful conclusion. The banker's strategy from the beginning is to foreclose and sell the collateral; often, the sooner this is done, the better and fewer assets will be dissipated. In the beginning, the bank and the business have the same goal: the business needs to turn around and make enough money to repay the bank loan. Who is in control depends on the size of the loan compared to the assets. If the assets of the business exceed the bank loan, the bank is in control. If the assets are much less than the loan, the borrower is in control. The greater the assets, the more money the bank can lose and the more power the borrower has, even to the extent of getting a greater loan from the bank.

UNDERSTANDING THE WORKOUT BANKER'S POSITION

Workout bankers are in the business to make money; however, positive economic value is not always mutually agreed between the bank and the borrower. When these situations don't go smoothly, banks assess economic value by interest and fee income. When a loan moves forward to a workout position, the bank starts to incur additional costs attributable to the loan even if the company is still paying the interest and/or fees. This put the workout banker's focus not on the top-line, but rather on the bank's overall profit and loss position. They get paid based on their overall performance with respect to the bank's bottom line, and the individual pay and compensation usually reflect the success of their decisions based on the loans in their portfolio.

RISK AGAINST CAPITAL REQUIREMENTS

Banks have a risk-adjusted profitability model that determines and measures loan contributions and profitability. A bank's traditional cost of sales is its financial capital, which is a key driver for loan profitability. This is defined by how much capital an individual loan consumes. The more capital deployed to a particular loan, the greater the fees and interest on the loan are required to cover the cost of capital for the bank to be profitable.

HOW DO BANKS MEASURE LOAN RISK?

Banks have internal metrics that quantify the amount of risk assigned to every loan. As the payment performance of the borrower goes down, the risk ratings also decrease which in turn heightens its overall risk rating for the loan. The riskier the loan is rated, the more additional capital the bank must reserve against the loan in order to protect against a future loss. When the capital requirements associated with the loan increase, the expense increases as well. This is calculated by inputting the risk rating combined in the bank's metric profitability model. If the bank can't increase pricing, it will not allow the bank to offset the additional cost of capital needed.

This means that when a borrower is having difficulty, the bank might increase the interest rate, which, from a normal perspective, does not make sense.

NON-PERFORMING ASSETS AND LOSSES

A non-performing loan is a loan that is 90 days past due, or loans which the bank doubts collectability. The borrower doesn't have to miss a payment to be classified in this way. If the bank thinks the loan is probably going to be a loss, then the bank would consider labeling the loan as non-performing.

Non-performing loans cause a bank to be hit twice on the bank's bottom-line profit; the bad loans reduce revenues and drive expenses up.

Losses, known as charge-offs, are negative factors that drive decisions when a loan is in a workout. The bank treats the loans the same as a company's accounts receivable. If the loan isn't repaid, then the bank calculates a dollar-for-dollar loss. The banks carry a reserve for losses, but when the individual loan risk profile deteriorates, the reserves and the expenses increase.

THE WORKOUT BANKER'S PERSPECTIVE

Understanding the economic impact of capital requirements, non-performing loans, risk ratings, and loan losses provides the reasons why workout bankers make the decisions that they do. This explains why a bank won't loan more on a bad loan. As the loan progresses up the risk spectrum, the attention it commands from both inside and outside the bank skyrockets. Riskier loans require more frequent and more detailed reporting. Auditors and regulators, both external and internal, will review the file and management wants to participate in the decisions. These riskier loans carry a lot of personal risk for the workout banker who arranged the loan, and they can be fired if they have a poor and underperforming portfolio. The administrative issues of a bad loan are huge, and the personal responsibility and "hassle factor" is always on the banker's mind.

WHY WERE YOU PUNISHED FOR A WORKOUT BANKER'S BREAKDOWN?

There are two places that are gold for buying a business at steep discounts – from workout people and a subsidiary of a parent company in bankruptcy. If you want to buy a discounted business to acquire the assets and sell them right away, run, do not walk to your nearest workout person and buy them lunch. Tell them what you're looking for and that you are ready to take that debt off their books.

There are ways to get the debt off the bank's books. The bank will usually be over secured, meaning if they liquidated all the assets, they would be profitable. In other words, the assets are worth more than the outstanding balance of the loan.

1. You can get a loan from another bank to remove the company from the bank's books.

2. You could refinance the bad loan with the same bank.

3. You could get an option on the company's assets and set up a sale. Sell the equipment, factor the receivables, sell the customers to a competitor all done at the same time and this is cash in your pocket.

Look for and buy companies in bankruptcy and which have subsidiaries.

INSOLVENCY AND BANKRUPTCY

Insolvency is another term for a company losing a lot of money or one going into bankruptcy currently or imminently. The difference between insolvency and bankruptcy is:

- Insolvency is a financial state meaning they lack the ability to pay debts.

- Bankruptcy is a legal process that finds the final solution to insolvency, the legal declaration of the inability to pay the debt.

Bankruptcy can solve insolvency by selling the insolvent business.

WHERE CAN YOU BUY AN INSOLVENT BUSINESS?

Running a business isn't easy, and changing economic times and situations challenge even the best small business owners. Poor and inadequate management usually causes insolvency, however, that is not the only reason. Insolvency can end an era for many owners and bring opportunities for others.

Finding an insolvent business requires planning. Although choosing the best business target can take time, finding insolvent companies should not be too difficult. Use an Internet search. Use terms like "Insolvent business", "failed companies", and "businesses in administration." You could even contact legal firms that handle insolvencies and bankruptcy cases.

THE BENEFITS AND RISKS OF BUYING AN INSOLVENT BUSINESS

Like starting any business, purchasing an insolvent business has advantages and disadvantages. You need to understand the benefits, along with risks. Insolvent businesses could mean companies losing a lot of money and are on their way out of business or a business that is in bankruptcy. An administrator is named for companies not in bankruptcy and a trustee is named for the ones in bankruptcy.

THE BENEFITS OF BUYING AN INSOLVENT BUSINESS

The biggest benefit of buying an insolvent business is that it is usually cheaper than starting from nothing because the assets are discounted, and you have immediate cash flow. An insolvent business has advantages, such as an existing customer base and readily available assets. These can assist in increasing your chances of success because you will not have to spend initial capital on these items.

The administrators want to find someone willing to take the business over, either by selling or liquidating the assets. A prospective buyer is usually welcomed in these situations. The buying process involves a lot of paperwork and legal hoops, but generally, it is quick, as the administrators want to dump the business as soon as possible. There are certain advantages that make purchasing an insolvent company advantageous. Usually, the old liabilities are left with the insolvent debtor, which means you can start relatively free of debts.

THE RISKS OF BUYING AN INSOLVENT BUSINESS

Keep in mind that you are buying a failing business. This means you don't know whether it is inherently flawed so that you will never make money. Depending on the structure of the deal, you might inherit liability that could hamper future gains. Determine what business assets and liabilities are part of the sale. For example, most insolvent companies require the purchaser to maintain the existing employment contracts. This means you will not be able to lay off employees right away or you might have to keep incompetent employees.

In a lot of these situations, there is not a lot of time to do due diligence and proper checks. This will increase the risk; it is possible you might not have enough time to review all the important aspects of the business.

THE BEST APPROACH TO BUYING AN INSOLVENT BUSINESS

Timing is important when buying an insolvent business, therefore the approach needs to incorporate the right mindset and plan. Starting a business by buying an insolvent business is a creative strategy that requires quick thinking and fast research but being methodical will speed and ease the transition.

CONSIDER THE TIMING

The first thing to consider is timing. With insolvent companies, everything moves fast; if you want to have the best deal, act fast. Before purchasing, select a target industry or business type. It's not like going shopping at the mall; businesses are not all equal and many should be liquidated. Once you find your target, it is time to move. Waiting too long can increase the risk of the company deteriorating further. If the business still operates with the original owner or operator, the risks are higher because you don't know for sure what is included and what is not. Anxiety runs through the employees, debtors, and creditors. This, by nature, will cause the business to suffer additional damage, which means more time, fewer assets.

Once the green light is on, be prepared and get any legal paperwork ready.

In short:

- When the company is in liquidation or administration, the current directors of the company have little said, and the administrator has the power to negotiate and execute a sale.

- If the business is in receivership, the administrator does not have the authority to pay unsecured creditors.

KNOW WHAT IS INCLUDED IN THE SALE

When you've identified the business, find out what is included in the sale in these three key areas:

- Liabilities – includes all financial liabilities and contractual liabilities. For example, check to see whether you are required to continue working with the same third-party operators and for how long.

- Warranties – lack of warranties is a significant risk when buying an insolvent business. Generally, you will not receive any warranties from the administrator. Good due diligence is important.

- Assets – depending on the process and the business, access to assets could be limited. Check all the assets, not just financial; create a list of what is included in the sale.

Besides the assets and liabilities, employee contracts could be the most crucial factor. This can increase your risk if the contracts are transferred to the new business. Otherwise, if employment contracts are canceled after the sale, you need a plan to hire new employees.

Verify each asset and liability and know what responsibilities the new company will be absorbing, such as financial, contractual, governmental or otherwise.

DO PROPER DUE DILIGENCE

Thorough due diligence is difficult to conduct when time is limited. Regardless, you should not ignore the usual checks of starting a new business.

When buying a business, whether it is insolvent or not, there are three aspects of due diligence:

- Legal due diligence – this covers most points discussed above.

- Financial due diligence – if the company has financial problems, it is important to understand what led to the failure.

- Commercial due diligence – it is important to know what type of market this business operates in and know the competition.

Know all your responsibilities after the business is transferred. This includes any legal documents required to conduct business.

CONSTRUCT A PLAN TO TURN THE BUSINESS AROUND

This is the most essential element for the future: a strong and effective plan that you can execute as soon as you take control. An effective plan is critical because it builds the road map to achieve success, especially because the company has been a loser. Take time to know the key decisions that led to its downfall. More than likely, you will implement changes in the way the business operates. Do not shy away from instituting and implementing your own vision of how the company can operate and be a success.

PROTECT YOURSELF AGAINST A FRAUDULENT TRANSFER CHALLENGE

If assets from a distressed company are purchased prior to a bankruptcy, the buyer is possibly at risk for a subsequent fraudulent transfer challenge. Under federal law, state law and/or the Bankruptcy Code, the sale can be avoided (i.e., set aside) upon dissatisfied creditors or by a bankruptcy trustee subsequent to a bankruptcy filing showing that there was "actual" fraud (i.e., the sale was actually intended to hinder, delay or defraud creditors) or, more likely, "constructive" fraud (i.e., the sale was made for less than fair consideration or reasonably equivalent value, and the target was insolvent at the time of or rendered insolvent by, the sale. Section 544 of the Bankruptcy Code permits a trustee to look back on these types of transfers for "reach-back" periods of six years or more. To reduce the risk, a buyer must do two things: (i) build the best conceivable record that "fair consideration" or "reasonably equivalent value" was paid and (ii) require that (A) the sale proceeds stay with the target and not be distributed to the target's stockholders and/or (B) adequate arrangements are made to pay-off the target's creditors.

SIGN AND CLOSE SIMULTANEOUSLY

An additional risk the buyer faces when acquiring the business in the non-bankruptcy situation is that the company could file Chapter 11 after the purchase agreement has been signed but before the actual transfer. If this happened, the business could "reject" the agreement, and the purchaser would have an unsecured, pre-petition claim against the company for damages. The company could "assume" the agreement and lock the buyer into a deal that may not look good after weeks of deterioration of the business. The way to eliminate this possibility is to sign and close simultaneously.

BANKRUPTCY CONTEXT

A Section 363 Sale is usually the best way to purchase. The purchase of assets from a Chapter 11 debtor may be done either (i) under Section 363 of the Bankruptcy Code (a "Section 363 Sale") or (ii) as part of the debtor's overall plan to reorganize. A Section 363 Sale is the more common method because it is easier and quicker, it avoids the plan having to be confirmed that incorporates disclosure and voting and minimizes the risk of a decline in value or a shortage of working capital. A Section 363 Sale is often more attractive than a non-bankruptcy acquisition for a number of significant reasons, including (i) in most cases, the bankruptcy court will approve the sale of the assets "free and clear" of all liens and liabilities (other than those liabilities that the buyer expressly agrees to assume and, arguably, certain "successor" liabilities, such as environmental and product liabilities claims); (ii) the approval of the bankruptcy court should bar any subsequent fraudulent conveyance challenges (as discussed above); (iii) the buyer will be able to cherry-pick assets and contracts (e.g., through the debtor's assumption/rejection rights discussed above) in ways not possible in the non-bankruptcy context and assumed contracts will be "cleansed" of non-assignability or change-of-control provisions (except for certain contracts, such as personal-services contracts and certain intellectual-property licenses); and (iv) State shareholder-approval laws and bulk-transfer laws generally do not apply to a Section 363 Sale.

A "PRE-PACK" MAY BE A GOOD ALTERNATIVE

Time is often the biggest risk when purchasing a company's assets in bankruptcy. The debtor's filing could activate negotiations with various creditors, unknown claims, litigation, etc. Therefore, a "prepackaged" Chapter 11 plan ("Pre-Packs") could be part of a Section 363 Sale. These are prevalent especially with the increased costs and the difficult to manage bankruptcy process under the Bankruptcy Abuse Prevention and Consumer Protection Act of 2005.

"Rule No. 1: Never lose money; rule No. 2: Don't forget rule No. 1."
– Warren Buffett, CEO of Berkshire Hathaway

For more information or get involved with us reach out to Jan Capital Inc. www.jancapitalinc.com

Chapter 3

JOINT VENTURES

"A business that makes nothing but money is a poor business." – Henry Ford, Founder of Ford Motor Company

JOINT VENTURES

Joint Ventures (aka Strategic Partnerships) often feel like pink elephants in the room. Very few people understand them or know how to profit from them. If you can understand this strategic leverage, it will change your business and bring the cash in.

Many people often want to be the boss and only the boss but what I've realized during business is that many great companies partner with similar businesses to accomplish goals. Jan Capital Inc is an investment company that I partnered with a former teammate Malik Zaire, and one of our main focuses was building joint ventures with others who have similar experiences or more knowledge than us because it makes the business venture more powerful.

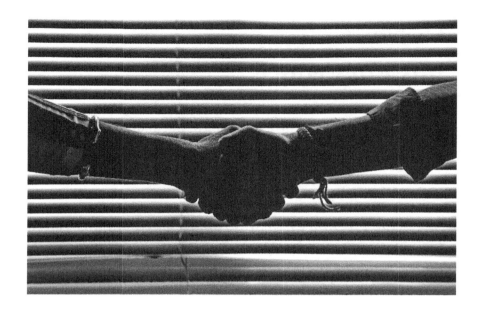

Joint ventures are great for people on all levels of business because when two people or entities collaborate on one common goal while using both sides resources make the chances of success much higher. From personal experience I've been able to be a part of three intriguing joint ventures that I thought I would never be doing but what made the opportunity special is because everyone had their strengths and weaknesses that helped everyone and that's one of most powerful benefits one receives by doing joint ventures instead of doing it all alone. After reading this book, talk to a friend/ family and take some time in a room and bounce ideas off each other and give the brain a chance to expand and come up ideas and solutions to them.

Even if one doesn't start the idea or bring it to market, the mental training component is good I'm sure you've heard of OPM (Other People's Money). But there's something much more powerful than OPM: OPA (Other People's Assets). You can easily access OPA, and they provide exponentially more opportunities and ROIs than just money. You can keep throwing money at something forever, but there's no guarantee that you'll get a return. But by nature, the usage of OPA is usually mutually beneficial, and it combines Operators. So, it magnifies your results.

To clarify, a joint venture involves two or more people or companies coming together to help each other maximize their earning potentials. It's a win/win: It combines a variety of potential Operators, who can develop to make money that neither of them would discover on their own. These business relationships can be extremely profitable.

In fact, joint ventures occur every day, and you might not even realize it. Many people have become multimillionaires by utilizing these strategies. The fastest, easiest and least risky ways to increase your profits involve leveraging off others' goodwill. What's the biggest advantage? You can utilize this strategy with little or no capital input, and massively grow your business overnight.

Almost instantaneously, you can develop a wide variety of new products and services. You can immediately acquire new knowledge and skills. Furthermore, you can make all kinds of money that you would never have made without the help and support of your joint-venture partners.

So, a joint venture is a shortcut to exploding your business with little to no risk. You're able to utilize other people's most profitable talents, skills, contacts, and Operators, which can help you make more money than ever before.

Joint ventures can add significantly more revenue and impact to any sales efforts your company pursues. If you're the middle person, you can bring in company concepts, ideas, and products that increase sales and profits.

Many times, this effort can be made with little cash, effort, extra people, or time commitment on either side. This lowers the barrier of entry. You can instantly be in a market that it takes most people years to break into, and it won't cost you a fortune. Also, you can quickly expand your company's customer base. If your company sells repeat or backend products, you could make a fortune—for no upfront risks whatsoever.

The biggest misconception about joint ventures is that they're complicated. While some can be complex and have a steep learning curve, many relationships are quite simple and don't require anything. You control the complexity upfront. The best thing you can do is to get started with a simple joint venture first, then save the more advanced ideas for later. Don't let fear stop you from using this compelling method to explode the profits of your business.

How to Get Started

You need a product or service, sales materials, and a list of customers who have done business with you in the past. Then, create a concept for your joint venture, contact your potential partner, and make an agreement. Next, create the offer for your customers and contact them. You contact everyone on your joint customer list, or you can divide it between you and your partner.

There are many ways to offer your target customer your product or service. A joint venture isn't a one-way street; it can go both ways.

Some Examples

A realtor could partner with a lawn service, cleaning service, or moving service. If customers use the realtor's people, they get a discount, and/or the realtor gets a finder's fee.

A hair salon could partner with a tanning salon, makeup shop, weight-loss product supplier, or any beauty- related business. They could offer discounts to their joint customers and pay their joint-venture partners a commission.

A distributor who has a customer base can immediately put comparable products in their distribution channel. Then their joint-venture partner could do a consignment inventory and get paid when their partner gets paid. (A manufacturer or any other company that has a customer base could do the same thing.)

The possibilities are endless.

What Are the Biggest Mistakes?

The #1 mistake people make is getting wrapped up in the theory. The second is that they get intimidated. The third is starting by going after a deal that's too big. They want to land the 400-pound whale, as opposed to landing a smaller fish and feeding their family and then working their way up to feeding the entire village.

You must be able to work through everything you do. You must start very small and maintain a tight focus on your company niche, then build your knowledge, expertise, and relationships.

You'll get rejected many times. Since the other side won't understand what you're trying to do, they may view it as a competitive strategy. But if you keep hammering away, you'll find the prospect you need, and you can build your record from this.

Minimize Your Risks Upfront

The biggest mistake you'll ever make in business is taking too much risk upfront on any deal, sale, or transaction. The risk could be capital, cash, relationships, sales, expenses, time, or too many benefits for others. The list goes on and on.

Las Vegas was built by risk-takers willing to invest their hard-earned money with hopes of getting rich quick. But how many people do you think leave Las Vegas with a profit? Very few! So don't treat your business-like Las Vegas.

Most business owners never assess their actions before they take them. In other words, they fall in love with an idea, concept, product, service, or person, and they become blind to the results.

One time, I had this great idea about a product. I asked people about it, and they loved it. I was ready to pay for molds and inventory and make an investment of about $140k. When the inventory arrived, I was so excited about selling it.

Unfortunately, the cost for the product was what I could sell it for in the market. I should have taken orders first, based on a prototype unit. Then I could have found out if it would sell profitably. I asked around and did market surveys, but people would just agree. So, the information was skewed. If I'd placed a real order, I would have known that they were only giving me "lip service." It was a hard lesson to learn, and it cost me $140k.

I could have invested that $140k in other products that were selling, and I would have gotten a good margin. Instead, I got a negative return on the money. How many mistakes can you make and still stay in business?

Always assess the risk/reward. Remove your emotions from the transaction and focus on the best results for the minimum amount of risk. A risk can involve both time and capital. If you spend your business's time dealing with problems and putting out fires, you can't get that time back. If you took that time and focused on building your business, the rewards could be massive.

Now I've literally written a book about each one of my biggest mistakes below. My goal is to give you enough information to trigger a thought, idea, or strategy that causes you to do research, understand the concept, and follow through in a way that allows you to make your business more profitable.

Always weigh your risk/reward in your business functions and strategy. Mistakes can be as simple as hiring customer service reps that don't like people, hiring incompetent people, and spending too much on expenses without getting a return. (Side note: Rule #1 in customer service is hiring customer service reps who like people. You'd be surprised how many don't.)

Do Something

It's not difficult to build a business with sound marketing strategies, but most people fail to execute them. They get started, but it doesn't go their way right away. They don't make money within a week. Then they get sidetracked by "life," and the business goes by the wayside. Then they find themselves in the same place doing the same things and getting the same results—month after month. All while they're stuck in a low-paying job they can't quit.

You can break out of this trap by taking a small step and slowly building from it. Then you'll get addicted to this process, and your business will explode.

One impediment to starting this process is encountering too much information. Millions of ideas and strategies *could* work, but they all have a foundation in common: do something. Don't get caught up in analysis paralysis.

A second impediment is not executing. When it doesn't work, modify it. When that doesn't work, try a new strategy. Keep modifying until you find a breakthrough that will explode your business.

Thomas Edison did over 10,000 experiments on the light bulb. When people asked him why he was still experimenting when he was in the 9,000's, instead of getting discouraged, he said that he now knew over 9,000 strategies that didn't work.

"Business opportunities are like buses, there's always another one coming." – Richard Branson, Founder of Virgin Group

For more information or get involved with us reach out to Jan Capital Inc. www.jancapitalinc.com

Chapter 4

FIND THE BANK, GET THE MONEY

There is always someone who is looking to do business with one some else because they may have one piece of the puzzle but need a partner for the other remaining piece of it. In other words, if you have a product for your business or have an idea but need money to build out the plan, there are plenty of banks and hard lenders who will loan the money for your business to help you take it to the next level. It will take some work on the business owner's end to make sure the business plan, projections and expenses are to show the lender that you're serious and can make a financial return for everyone involved. Again, as you think through different scenarios or opportunities to gain capital to grow your business, it can be good to shop around different banks/lenders to see which options work best with your business structure and plans.

One of the first things you hear growing up is that "it takes money to make money." This saying is true because nothing comes from nothing. However, the money doesn't always have to come from you.

It's important to understand that you're trying to reach your end goal—because just throwing money at something doesn't mean it will be successful. Throwing money at it means the money comes from somewhere, so it needs to be recouped or repaid, and you need to make a profit.

When you need money, here's the question to ask: What will you do with it? Never take money without a plan that you can successfully execute to get a return on it. Suppose you have a product, and you're at manufacturing capacity. You're still unable to fill the orders. If you approach a similar manufacturer to make it for you, you can sell it. Then you'll expand your market and make more profit, and so will the manufacturer.

Another opportunity could involve selling a special type of shirt, and you have limited customers. You could borrow $100k and build a customer base through marketing. Maybe this endeavor increases sales, or you could lose all the money. Another possibility involves approaching a business that has customers but no shirt like yours, so you offer it to their customers. These examples are simple, but the concept and possibilities have endless opportunities.

Of course, sometimes you need cash flow, and the least risky way is to use other people's money (OPM). But you should first exhaust all possibilities of leverage before venturing into OPM—because the risk is lower, and the upside is greater. Tapping into a distribution channel that can generate immediate results could take millions of dollars and years to build. But if you can get into it in a brief period, the potential results could save you years, heartache, and money.

One thing you will find out the more you network with other businesspeople is that everyone is always looking for the next big business model. Having a great business structure and plan on how you will bring revenue will be a fantastic way for a traditional bank or even investors to deuce to toss a ton of money your way for your business to flourish. Once you have one or two people on board to give you capital towards your business venture, you then go show proof of concept of how you're able to expand the more capital backing the business receives. A solid financial plan with proof of concept will give business owners the opportunity to receive money from the bank without having to give up a piece of the company.

LEVERAGE IS BETTER THAN CASH

Money makes the world go round. Without it, you'll have no place to live and nothing to eat, which would be terrible. Since you're supposedly a small business owner, homelessness is probably not your situation. But to get started, grow, or survive, you must have capital; we can agree on that fact.

Some of the most successful people didn't always have cash as their capital, but had relational cash, asset, marketing, and good old-fashioned ingenuity (capital, not actual money).

The first thing you must ask yourself is what you're going to do with the borrowed money. What is it going to provide? If the money is just going to pay your monthly bills and get you through a brief period, it's not worth it. Don't do it.

Instead, tighten your belt. Sell what you must or work for someone else. I know you don't want to hear that. But if you can't realize a return of substantial value for the cash investment, find another way.

Most small business owners don't understand financing. We live in a society where every bank is trying to get you to borrow money. Most people believe that the only way to grow their business is by borrowing more money in the hopes of recouping the loan. But what happens is the debt keeps growing, which drives the expenses up and will eventually kill the business.

Small business owners understand this fact and don't take unnecessary loans. So, they leverage other capital first. Do they borrow it? Sometimes. But they only borrow when they can calculate a sufficient return based on the cash input. Here's what they do instead: leverage their assets. When they do this, the results are not 1+1=2. It's more like 1+1=3.

I know this concept might seem complicated, but once you understand it, you'll maximize your business and explode your profits. There are some basic concepts, but they vary, depending on the business, product, and situation.

Defining Leverage

eBay's website auction is a platform that provides the opportunity for people with products to sell, and they reach many people. eBay has many people viewing their website every day looking for products, which expands the seller's customer base and range. The seller is using leverage by listing products on eBay, and everyone wins: the seller, the buyer, and eBay.

AirBnB's website reservation is a platform that can connect people who have property they want to rent out to people who are looking for a short-term place to stay. AirBnB has many people viewing their website every day looking for rooms to rent. The homeowner is using leverage by listing their space on Airbnb, and everyone wins: the seller, the buyer, and Airbnb.

Kickstarter's crowdfunding platform connects inventors who

want funding for their products with individuals who want to invest in innovative products before they're placed on the open market. The inventors on Kickstarter can presell their items before they're made, but they're lacking funds to produce their viable ideas.

They can go to Kickstarter and leverage off their base of buyers. Again, everyone can win, but there are more risks in this situation. If the inventor has an innovative idea, it can be stolen and sold by someone else before he or she can sell it. Many predators monitor websites like Kickstarter to steal ideas.

With the above leverage, the providers charge a fee for the transaction that's facilitated between the buyer and the seller. Airbnb, eBay, and Kickstarter all operate this way, and they make billions of dollars from these platforms.

Let's break this concept down a little more. Here's the question you should ask: If you had the money, what would you do with it? Expand manufacturing? For example, you have sales and cannot keep up with the manufacturing. So, your problem is someone else's solution. You can go to a non-competitor who has a similar manufacturing capability and arrange for them to manufacture your product for you.

LOW-RISK MAX RETURN

The risk is usually lower for both sides. If you borrow $100k, you can lose it all. If you borrow someone's customer base that costs millions to acquire and years to refine, it could cost you nothing upfront. And you have zero risks.

To get a better understanding, let's go through some examples...

A smart Operators attorney had an office with empty office space. He had the infrastructure, a paralegal, and a fully functioning and efficient office. He wanted to scale back on his workload, and he was turning people away. He brought in a younger attorney who had been paying for their own office and made a deal; the older attorney would provide the office, paralegal, and client referrals and receive a percentage of the young attorney's business. He made an extra $75k; the other attorney made an additional $125k and everyone won.

A medical doctor and a dentist cross-utilized their patient base; they were also underutilizing the facilities. The medical doctor sent a letter to his patients referring them to the dentist, who was offering a free checkup to all new patients for a limited time. The dentist did the same thing with his patients, offering free medical checkups for new patients. The dentist picked up 42 new patients, and the doctor picked up 51 new patients.

An inventor of an effective weight-loss product approached a weight loss supplement company and made a deal with them to send an endorsement ad to their current customers offering a discount on the new product. They each made over 1 million dollars.

A deli was looking for more delivery business at lunchtime, and they were surrounded by several large offices. The deli owner visited the offices and offered the boss and the receptionist a free lunch once a week if someone else in their office ordered from the deli. He also offered a 10% discount on all orders. The deli owner built a route where he would visit one of 35 offices one day a week and increased his sales dramatically.

A lawn care company had a route consisting of 200

customers. They wanted to generate more income but were limited in their capability. They contacted companies that provided pool, carpet cleaning, power washing, and bug spray services and arranged for special prices for his homeowner customers. He generated an additional $40,000 in referral fees.

A real estate agent created relationships with a repair company, a cleaning company, a moving company, a finance company, and a promotional product company. The real estate agent generated over $50,000 a year in additional income.

A medical supply company selling a specialty prosthetic leg unit had a good relationship with the doctors. The staff at the doctors' offices found a supplier of braces for the prosthetic leg unit which increased their bottom line by over $1 million dollars.

A travel service created a relationship with a hotel chain that had empty rooms, a cruise line that had empty cabins, and a radio station. The travel service traded the hotel rooms and empty cabins for advertising on the radio station. The radio station gave the rooms and cabins away as prizes. The travel agent sold the hotel rooms and cabins for the regular price and received a commission. Everyone won in this deal.

One smart Operators knew of a company that gave and sold seminars to businesses for strategic and effective ways to create profits. Before they made the change, they were marginally profitable. They found a person who had authored a book that wasn't selling but was an informative book on a subject that fit their market. They connected the two, and they presented a seminar and recorded it. This, combined with the book, created better credibility and stronger marketing material which allowed them to present seminars out of their area and each made over 1 million dollars.

A public speaker partnered with booking agencies. The agencies receive a portion of the fees, and the speaker refined his speech and authored the books. The speaker might get paid a small amount for the engagement but could offer the books and material at the back of the room.

UNDERSTANDING JOINT VENTURES

A leveraged relationship could be called a joint venture or arbitrage, and simply put, it is an arrangement between two or more businesses where each party brings something of value to the other party, such as space, capability, customers, reputation, and much more. The overall objective is to leverage both sides' assets and join them together to get a maximized return. Joint ventures employ leverage where the assets or property influence both businesses; this is usually the objective where both companies will benefit. Normally, when employing leverage, each joint venture would be responsible for their costs, losses, and profits. The joint venture remains separate from each of the other's respective business interests. Joint ventures will often combine their business relationships to aid in diversifying assets when compared to their own product offerings.

BUNDLED PRODUCTS AND SERVICES OF THE JOINT VENTURE

One way to maximize the respective leverage of the joint ventures to help small businesses is bundling the company's products and/or services with that of the other joint venture partner to expand the product offering with like or synergistic items that will make up a "package deal" that improves the needs of the customer and creates more revenue for both companies. This can reduce costs for your business while expanding the opportunity to gain a large profit boost while serving your customer base better. An example of this could be a diet book combined with supplements, and/or an exercise program. It could be someone selling bath towels and including specialty soap. They could sell shoes and add socks and/or shoelaces, foot cream, foot massages, and more.

Smart Operators #5

These smart Operators owned a car wash, which had a great sales strategy: It was able to get almost all customers to upgrade to a hot wax. The strategy brought in thousands of extra dollars every month. They licensed the selling strategy to 2,000 other car washes for $100 a month.

If you have a great selling or manufacturing strategy, evaluate whether it's competitive to you. If it's not, license it to others that are out of your area and make the money on your valuable technique!

PARTNER JOINT VENTURES BY ENDORSEMENT

There are several opportunities to gain attention and market share through influencers and endorsers. They can give instant credibility by combining their relationships with a product or service. This leverages the relationship of the partner who has the end customers. If the customer gets a letter, email or phone call and they have a relationship with that company they will buy increasingly often. A typical deal will be with products and services within the same industry, such as a sandwich shop offering a drink, a rental company offering labor, a doctor providing the prescriptions and on and on.

Bring the right products to your customers and it can increase your customer loyalty and your profits. Letting your customers know they will be best served by using your products or services along with those of your partners is an effective strategy. There are several ways this can work if the company offers a complimentary product: the endorser could receive a commission, or they could buy the product and offer it to their customer base and make a greater margin or earn a referral fee; the possibilities are endless.

DEVELOPING A NEW PRODUCT OR SERVICE

Leveraging partners carries many distinct levels of sophistication, experience, and expertise. Managing these re-Operators and combining knowledge and access can create a huge opportunity for the small business owner. The small business might have an excellent product that could sell in a market but doesn't have the money to execute a sales strategy.

The small business owner could contact the larger company and pitch the idea. An example is a unique exercise item that an app exercise company could plug into their distribution or vice versa the exercise machine seller could offer the app to their customers. The possibilities are endless, and they could collaborate on a new product and take that to the customer base as well.

MARKETING AND ADVERTISING CO-SHARED

Marketing campaigns are a different animal, and they create an opportunity to cross-utilize the marketing dollars with a partner. This could be as simple as running an event sponsored by a large fitness company and joining the venue and capturing some of their customers. For example, during a Cross-fit event, you could sell muscle cream for tired athletes. It could be an online program generating leads and driving those leads to a website with complementary products.

A small business owner must be creative and savvy to pull this off but once you do it, even just the first one, you have a track record and can pull off many. Like anything else, practice and experience make it easier and better.

CO-SPONSORING AN EVENT

There are huge opportunities in cosponsoring with a partner. A larger partner will allow more exposure. It could be something as simple as a weight loss practitioner presenting clinics and offering a free lunch, and you could offer a non-competing product such as pain relief.

HOW CAN YOU GRAB THE RING?

Leverage and understanding are vital in taking advantage of the opportunity. The leverage strategy is way beyond just sales, using and employing it provides the real multiplier effect. There are 3 common elements that cross all industries:

- Offer products and services, which will increase marketing, sales, and customer service.

- Complete and integrate the procurement, shipping, and delivery of the product.

- Plan and control the entire process including the technology of the product or the venue, the staff needed, and the funds.

Find the right partners for each opportunity and process. Know the area you want to leverage.

Determine who has what you lack. Remember your problems are someone else's solutions.

Attack and create a relationship. You might have to go through several potential partners before you get one that is willing to cooperate. Don't worry about that. This concept is extremely high level, and most small businesses would feel threatened, but once they do it, they will do so repeatedly.

The easiest and most overlooked way is to cross-leverage sales channels with products or services. The primary objective is to maximize results with minimal time and effort. This can be achieved with leverage: creating large returns with minimal risk and investment.

The first step is to identify the product or service that you want to market. Second, is to find the potential partners with a distribution process that makes the most sense and is compatible with your product. Can you get past the gatekeeper to pitch the idea? Is this a one-off deal or a continuous deal that can bring in long-term revenue? Can you do multiple deals with the same partner, or do you need multiple partners? One venture with one partner can make you hundreds of thousands of dollars.

You must understand the principal issue up front - efficiency versus effectiveness. If you are efficient, you could possibly do many deals and none make any money, but if you are effective, you could do one deal and make millions. Focus your time on finding an effective partner; add value to them, get more sales and profits, and then you can expand from there.

Leverage is what business is all about. If you could take only one concept away - it would be to understand this; it is not only where the money is - it is where the growth is. Instead of you being one small business, you can use leverage and have the power of a business ten times your size. And once you flex that muscle, you will increase your bottom line many times the size it is now.

THE OPERATORS AND OPM

In the business world, you've heard, "You must have money to make money." There are endless ways to get money. However, the best one to use for your business is other peoples' money (OPM).

One of the best "insider secrets" of the most successful people on the planet is summed up in those three words: Other People's Money - OPM for short. If you took a survey, you would find that most successful people used OPM in one form or another. You'll see that they were propelled into making fortunes utilizing OPM. The utilization of other individuals' cash has turned out to be an ethical and acceptable avenue in business and it's a normal practice. You can use other people's cash and leverage it to your advantage.

For instance, you can use borrowed cash to buy into high

return yield programs that could create a great return to pay back your moneylender and fill your pockets too. Or you can use OPM and turn it into an asset producing or income-producing re-Operators that you will eventually own debt-free. Or you can use OPM to develop your business. The advantages of utilizing OPM are self-evident:

1) When you utilize OPM, particularly inside the parameters of your company, your debt and liability can be allocated to the business, and you would not be personally liable.

2) With the increase in cash, you can grow the business and make more profits.

Grabbing hold of the OPM is a type of leverage that expands your own assets and individual abilities. The leverage of others' assets and your own assets is the key to success with any business. Leverage is not just about money to buy other assets. Facilities, customers, relationships, and just about anything can be leveraged. This knowledge is the key that separates a normal business from the ones that can take advantage of OPM and maximize their business. The money opens more doors and allows the ability to acquire more assets to drive more profit.

WHAT THE WEALTHY DO

The wealthiest individuals on the planet have always known about utilizing OPM. Bill Gates, Warren Buffet, Donald Trump, and many others have exceeded expectations with this rule. Their ability to use OPM to acquire assets and re-Operators is unbelievable. Individuals approach building an empire or obtaining re-Operators in several ways with their experience and past relationships with the help of OPM. Generally, individuals consider vast wealth and riches unattainable; they do not believe that it is possible for them, especially on the backs of someone else's cash. What a great many people fail to understand is that you really don't need cash to make a profit; what you need is the re-Operators that the OPM can deliver.

OPM buys you time; it empowers you to get things done faster than you would otherwise. It permits you to take advantage of opportunities your own assets don't allow you to do. It empowers you to make decisions you couldn't normally. It takes the average individual many years to gather riches or construct a business completely using their own assets. With OPM, you quickly increase your leverage for building personal and business wealth and can accelerate the growth of your business.

Most people's first experience with OPM is when they buy a home and get a mortgage. Ordinarily, their down payment, income history, and credit score decide whether they can get a home loan. Your house isn't your asset; it is an asset of the bank. The bank is making money off their money, not you. Getting a bank to give you a loan for a rental house, this becomes an investment property. This is an asset based on OPM. When you use OPM, it is the bank's money that generates income. The rental income not only pays the mortgage but also pays you a profit and once the mortgage is paid off, you are way ahead of the game.

In business, entrepreneurs gain admittance to OPM when they write a marketable strategy and present it to the money people. This is commonly called "raising capital". As a byproduct of getting the cash (known as capital), the investor will usually get a large payback or equity in the deal/transaction of the business. Money can be from a bank, the bank gets paid back the principal amount with interest, which allows them to make a profit. Too many bad loans and they are out of business. It's the small business owner's responsibility to put the cash flow to effective use and deliver items or produce income to pay back the loan. Do not borrow money from a bank just to pay living expenses; only borrow or raise money on income-producing items, strategies, or tactics.

OPM is accessible and open to the financially stable. Your first obligation is to understand the risks and opportunities of OPM and the various structures that use OPM. OPM is the key and utilizing OPM is not without its traps. Like each money related exchange, there are characteristic dangers. In the first place, you are subject to reimburse the capital acquired and pay interest. The important thing is to understand that OPM can empower you to maximize your current position and business. Most small business owners are over-anxious about seizing every opportunity to use OPM and that is a huge mistake. It's important to choose the right opportunity and make it work. I know one dishonest businessman (I won't call him an Operator), was trying to make a product and raised over $500k from many different Operators and never made the product in over five years. He continues to pitch; surprisingly, no one has put him out of his misery.

Business is built like any other structure —with a solid foundation, sturdy frame, inside walls, hurricane proof windows, and a nice paint job; but each building and business has its unique characteristics and opportunities. Without a proper structure, your building will collapse. So will your business. You need to have a good plan that can be implemented when you are seeking OPM.

IT'S ALL ABOUT THE STORY

The main thing to know when seeking OPM, building a business, or getting a date, is all about the story: specifically, details about why, how and who are convincing. In today's terms, it is known as a pitch deck. Individuals often are confused by the expression "Story"—they believe it's just about running around and telling tall tales or leaving out genuine materials and the facts.

Stories have been around for as long as language; people of all ages can relate to a story. We learn through stories and parables. Stories capture attention, catch emotion and influence thoughts—to be able to pitch for money; you must have a story that is real and effective. Not every story and pitch are the same for everyone you will meet; you need to tailor your story to your audience. There is a particular structure that is used to make a remarkable story.

HOW TO STRUCTURE THE STORY

- What is the problem in the market – the bad guy of the story?
- What is the solution – The "good guy" of the story?
- How will the good guy kill the bad guy?
- The Business Plan – How does the good guy navigate the landscape?
- What are the Benefits? –Show why this is the best solution to the problem

- Decide the audience – is it a business, consumer, or others? Whoever it may be, explain the benefits to them.

- Current Status - where are you and what have you done? List the milestones you've achieved. This must include awareness that has been created, a description of the product, users, sales, influencers, testimonials, etc. Include anything that paints the picture and tells a compelling story.

- Market Analysis—prove the overall strength of the market and the trends. Quantify how you can be a player in the market and take market share – show the potential and how you will snag it.

- Opportunities—describe the trends of the market, and most importantly; why you and why now? What is the business model—how do you plan to make money?

- Projections and the financial future.

- How are you going to market your product and what strategies will you employ to stand out?

- What is your competition? List the primary competitors; start with the largest and work your way down. Also, show how you are unique and have an advantage. Do not bad mouth the competitor; only show how you are different in a positive way.

- Your management group—List the executives, their experience and associations. Make sure you have some ability in the product or service in the industry.

- The strategy you will use. What are the milestones and how will you achieve them? Name the product or service, the marketing aims and sales projections for the next year, two years and three years.

- What added growth opportunities are there? Include new products, services, or markets that you can capture showing enormous potential for growth. What are you looking for—how much money is needed and how will it be used?

A successful Operator running a small business has learned one of two things - leverage and using OPM. Whenever they need to expand, generate income, get a deal or tap into someone else's assets they have mastered these fundamentals.

The small business owner normally starts their business the old-fashioned way - they take the most personal risk by using their own money, credit cards, home loan or money from friends and family. By comparison, the Operators hardly ever use their own money, even if it is a startup. They not only target and use banks but several other cash Operators as well. The smart operator has an image in the market; he appears to be successful which creates credibility. In today's Internet world it is easy to give this feeling by creating a website and social media site which can create instant credibility and open the coffers of OPM. Once you develop the story and create the backdrop, you will have instant credibility – you will be a player in the market. Image feeling is the key for credibility. Many years ago, it was harder to get instant credibility. A reference or referral was one of the few ways to get fast credibility, and while those are still tried and true ways, in today's digital age, the feeling is instant and if the presentation is well done, you look credible immediately.

GET SOME CASH

If you have no credit or poor credit this is a problem because many will perceive that as a high-risk investment business opportunity. They ask themselves, "Can I trust them? Are they going to be paying their living expenses with my money?" With a low credit score, it is hard to raise cash especially from standard lending institutions that traditional Operators use. If you've been turned down for a loan or don't want to get stuck paying high, subprime interest rates, here are some alternatives to consider:

If you have enough equity in your property, you can get a low-interest, tax-deductible line of credit to spend any way you want. Tapping into your home equity puts your property in jeopardy if you can't repay the debt. If you have a reliable income and are disciplined about paying down an equity line, it's an inexpensive choice, regardless of your credit score.

APPLY TO CREDIT UNIONS

Credit unions are like banks but are owned by their members who typically have something in common, work in the same industry or live in the same geographic area. Credit unions are nonprofit organizations that pass along earnings/savings to members in the form of lower fees.

GET A PEER-TO-PEER LOAN

Peer to peer or P2P lending has been around for a while now. It's an online platform that allows you to borrow directly from an individual instead of an institution. Right now, you can borrow for as little as 6%. These sites work in diverse ways, but the first step is to post a request for a loan and state why you need the money. Investors review loan listings and choose the ones that meet their criteria. Peer to peer lenders screen all applicants and check your credit, which becomes part of your loan listing. So, while your credit score is still a factor, an individual investor may be more sympathetic to your situation than a traditional bank.

Check out these peer-to-peer lending sites for borrowing or investing:

- Prosper

- Lending Club

- Perform

- SoFi

TAKE A LOAN FROM FAMILY OR FRIENDS

If an online peer doesn't lend to you, maybe family or friends will. Treat a loan from someone you know just like any business transaction. To avoid complications later, create a written agreement that includes the interest rate, payment terms, any collateral you are putting up for the loan, and what happens if you do not repay the debt. The bottom line is that a family loan must help everyone involved and should be your last resort.

APPEAL TO A COSIGNER

If you don't have a friend or family member who's willing or able to give you a loan, maybe one with good credit would be willing to cosign a loan for you. Someone who knows your situation and trusts your ability to repay the debt would probably be willing to take a chance on you. Just remember that if you default and don't repay the debt, the creditor will look to your co-signer for full payment. Additionally, all the payment history will be recorded on both of your credit reports, which could be devastating for your cosigner.

LOANS WITH NO CREDIT CHECK

Credit can often be overlooked. Many of us don't even consider our credit scores until we need to take out a personal or business loan. Only then do we understand the implications of our credit score. It can decide whether it's possible to buy a home, purchase a car, or even start our dream business. Whether you became aware of your credit score by a business loan denial, or you're just starting your search for business funding and already know your credit isn't quite excellent, you might be asking yourself where to find a small business loan that doesn't require a credit check. For traditional financing, which is impossible.

FINDING A BUSINESS LOAN WITH NO CREDIT CHECK

There are a few lenders, like Fundbox, that offer invoice financing with no hard credit check. They finance based on your business sales. It requires business sales and invoices to be given; this type of funding wouldn't be an option if you were just starting up and have no orders. You'll need at least three months of business history along with an outstanding sales invoice for this type of lender to be a choice. When a lender decides whether to lend money to your business, they're evaluating the risk that it may pose. They ask, "Will this borrower default on the loan?" If you have no history to prove that your business can run smoothly and no credit score to prove you're financially responsible, how can a lender know that you'll eventually pay your debt to them?

HOW TO FIND BUSINESS LOANS WITH BAD CREDIT

There are some lenders that just do a soft credit check—meaning it won't affect your credit score. If you're afraid you have "bad credit," make sure you understand the FICO score ranges before deciding that no lender would want to work with you. You might underestimate your credit score or your loan options. Lenders will typically consider your personal credit in the following tiers.

- 700 or Above

If you've got a credit score of 700 or higher, then you meet the minimum credit requirement for almost any kind of business funding, even the most difficult, like SBA loans or bank loans.

- 650 to 700

If your credit score falls somewhere between 650 and 700, then you're still in fairly good shape. In fact, after you get a bit of business history under your belt and your business is in good financial shape, you might still be able to qualify for an SBA loan with a credit score in this range.

- 620 to 650

When your credit score falls into the 620 to 650 range, that's when your options become a bit limited. That said, with a score like this, after a few months of business, you could still qualify for a medium-term loan from an alternative lender.

- 500 to 550

With a credit score that falls somewhere between 500 and 550, then you'll have a bit of trouble qualifying for a loan. That said, though your credit score won't help you in qualifying, that doesn't mean you don't have options. If you get a bit of business history under your belt, and you have some financial stats to show for it, then you could still qualify for certain types of short-term or secured funding.

- Below 500

If you've got a credit score that's below 500, your options for funding your business will be limited, and often less-than-ideal. If your score falls below 500, take time to improve your credit history before taking on business funding.

Your small business could be doing well overall. But an unexpected event could change everything. An incident of theft or accident could lead to an immediate need for cash that you might not have in the bank. You could miss out on a great business opportunity because you don't have enough money to buy supplies or to cover payroll. To further complicate matters, when you don't have strong personal or business credit, quickly securing a line of credit or short-term loan can be difficult and expensive.

If you're running into cash flow problems month after month, you'll likely need to take a serious look at your business and figure out a way to right your ship. But when you're in need of a one-time cash injection, consider the following options and advice:

ASK FOR TERMS FROM VENDORS

Rather than focusing on how to raise money right away, look for a way to minimize your expenses. Business owners can ask for terms from their vendors. If you have good relationships, they may be willing to let you pay with net-30, net-60 or even longer terms. Having an extra month or two to pay your bills could free up cash to cover an immediate need. Paying vendors early can help build your business's credit score. If your vendors don't agree to change terms, perhaps they'll accept installment payments on your current balances. Again, this isn't a long-term solution, but it could help free up money for a one-time expense.

Consider a variety of options that don't require high credit scores. Some lending options don't necessarily require a high personal or business credit score; review the terms, fees, and requirements, as they vary drastically for diverse types of funding and from one lender to the next.

LINE OF CREDIT

A line of credit is one of the most popular forms of working capital financing. These include a business credit line from a bank or an alternative lender, a business credit card, or a personal credit card or line of credit. Credit cards are a trendy way of dealing with everyday funding needs. But these typically have high-interest rates, so you should consider alternatives first.

FACTORING

Invoice financing lets you receive cash now for outstanding invoices. The fees can vary, and you should read the terms of the agreement carefully before signing with a factoring company. Some factoring companies offer more flexible terms including letting you choose which invoices you want to factor.

ONLINE BUSINESS LOANS

Some online lenders such as Kabbage may offer loans based on a business's performance, rather than your credit history. The interest rate will usually be higher than what you'd receive from a traditional bank loan, but the low credit requirement and effortless process make online lenders a worthwhile alternative to traditional bank loans. You might also be able to get the funds within a few days. Depending on the lender, you may be able to take out an installment loan or quickly open a line of credit and draw from it as needed.

MICRO-LENDING SERVICES

Look into micro-lending services, such as Kiva Zip. Although raising the money partially depends on your ability to promote your fundraising campaign, there's no credit-score requirement and loans through Kiva Zip have a 0% interest rate. Also, look for local Community Development Financial Institutions Funds (CDFI Funds) that provide micro-loans based on the business's accomplishments and owner's experience rather than credit scores.

MERCHANT CASH ADVANCES

Even with poor credit, business owners may be able to quickly receive a merchant cash advance, a loan that you repay with a part of your business's credit and debit card sales through automatic deductions from your business bank account. High-interest rates and daily or weekly repayment requirements could drastically eat into your company's cash flow and hinder your ability to run or grow the business.

PLAN AHEAD AND AVOID FUTURE PROBLEMS

Waiting until the last minute to look for funding can turn a slight problem into a major disaster. By planning ahead, you can ensure you'll have access to working capital when you must deal with an emergency or take advantage of a fantastic opportunity.

CROWDFUNDING

In recent years, Crowdfunding has become a popular choice for entrepreneurs looking to launch a new product or service. It lets you tap into the collective efforts of friends, family members, customers, and individual investors to raise the capital you need to start your business. Crowdfunding platforms like Indiegogo, Kickstarter, and GoFundMe make it easy for you to host an online campaign and reach potential backers through email and social media. Plus, there's the added benefit of confirming and refining your business concept through feedback from the masses.

There are a few types of Crowdfunding to consider when you're planning a campaign for your business:

Donation-Based

Donation-based Crowdfunding is when there is no incentive

for the backers. This is typically reserved for nonprofits, disaster relief, community projects, or medical bills/funeral expenses.

<u>Rewards-Based</u>

Rewards-based Crowdfunding offers backers a reward for contributing to your business typically in the form of a product or service that your company offers, or a special gift or experience to say thank you.

<u>Equity-Based</u>

Equity-based Crowdfunding gives backers the opportunity to become owners of the company by trading cash for shares. This means that they receive a financial return on their investment in your company.

SMALL BUSINESS GRANTS

Small business grants are excellent sources of funds because, unlike small business loans, you don't need to pay them back. You just need to qualify, which can be difficult. Many departments of government offer various grants from federal, state, and local agencies that can help a small business get started or expand. The catch is that they are typically reserved for specific industries and causes that have been found by the government, such as scientific or medical research or conservation efforts.

MICROLOANS AND NONPROFITS

If you're a minority small business owner or come from a disadvantaged background, you might qualify for a microloan or assistance from a nonprofit organization.

Generally, these options won't require you to prove creditworthiness, so a credit history that's limited or rocky won't necessarily hold you back from securing funding. These lenders aren't out for their financial benefit; they want to help traditionally marginalized groups and strengthen struggling communities, such as:

- Kiva U.S.

- Indiegogo

- PayPal Working Capital

- Square Capital

- Kickstarter

These types of financing are usually done without factoring the owner's personal credit.

CREATE AN EMERGENCY FUND

Just as many households keep a rainy-day fund and view it as an important part of their personal finances, business owners can also set up an emergency business fund. Make a practice of putting a part of your business's profits into a separate account that you can dip into during a crisis, or when the right opportunity presents itself.

Understand the business and reduce costs. Sometimes you should be working on your business rather than in it. Take an occasional step back and look for ways to improve your business's operations, find problems, and brainstorm solutions.

One smart operator had an idea about starting a vending

machine operation but had no money to do it. He discussed a strategy with a co-worker. The co-worker initially was cold to the idea, but the Operators took them to the locations that had vending machines and to ones that didn't and showed him the market. This allowed them to talk to the employees that were using vending machines and to employees working at companies that did not have the machines but wanted them. The co-worker bought in, and they created a partnership, built the business, and eventually sold it making a nice profit. The Operators found a profitable marketing niche, developed a plan to make money, didn't have the money but found a partner, pitched the partner, and went the extra step by showing him the opportunity by driving him around and, in the end, they both profited.

Key advice for one who is already in business or will be in the future

If you own a business, you know it is like your baby. It is you that either bought, inherited, or built it up, regardless, it is yours and you have put your blood, sweat, and tears into making your business what it is today.

Anyone can call you ugly but when they call the baby ugly most people get mad. It is that same way with your business, it is uniquely yours.

What is the key to maximizing growth and scaling while positioning your business for an exit enabling you to get the most amount of money?

It is about knowing when to sell and having good fundamental strategies and executing those strategies. It can be the difference from making a few hundred thousand dollars to making many millions or even billions. It really is that big of a difference.

About 50% of all businesses survive at the 5-year anniversary mark. About 30% of businesses make it to 10 years. A small business (for this definition under 100 people) make up 98.2% of all businesses and employ 59 million people and make up 44% of the economy in the United States, important and significant. What other industry or thing you can do that the longer you are in it, the greater chance of failure you have.

An important aspect when getting into a business is do I create a job for myself, or do I want to build the business and create wealth? The amount of time it takes to create a job or build massive wealth is the same. The separation is the strategy and execution.

As anyone in business knows it is never easy and takes a great amount of dedication, hard work and thick skin. My job is to show you how you can work, not in your business but on your business – sell or grow and sell business for more profits. How to get your money out of the business and how to get the most amount of money for your business on a sale.

Only 20% of businesses sell. With so many businesses in the United States, it is a competitive market. Not just competitive in the field of business selling products and services but competitive for you to cash out, especially getting the most out of what you have.

Most times the average business owner does not know or understand how to first sell their business and second maximize the selling price.

Most just throw it to a fast-talking business broker that wants to lock you into a contract whether they perform or not. Regardless of the business, the numbers don't work in your favor because 80% of all businesses never sell. The broker will lock you into a contract and put it on a website and just by pure volume and almost no work, they sell a few companies and yes, you guessed it they sold for less than what the hard-working owner should have received but they still get their commission.

But there is a formula to maximize the sale price.

First, you must know how much money you need out of the business on a sale and what your expectations - financially are and what do you need once you exit. If your business is worth $3 million dollars and you need $10 million dollars to keep your lifestyle to have the fun and enjoyment, you deserve.

Then you have a wealth gap. The difference between the $3 million current price and the $10 price you need is $7 million.

Second, if your business has a net income of $300,000. The income is usually calculated by the average income for the last 3 years, you multiply this by the standard industry selling multiple, which are industry standards, but not all businesses are equal. Let's say the multiple is 4 for your business which would make the business worth approximately $1.2 million.

Something to keep in mind and many people do not understand or know is that the multiples for a business sale have a range – from a low-end business to a high-end business, meaning that if the procedures and infrastructure are not good it would be classified as a low-end business. If the company can implement strategies and execute, the company could graduate all the way up to a "best in class" business where that multiple could be 4 which makes that business sell for approximately $3.6 million dollars. That is 4 times the profit for the same business. This is called a profit gap.

The third area is your personal plan and where do you see yourself in 3 years, 5 years, and beyond?

It is important to take these three factors into account in the beginning and revisit often. This will help drive your next key decision.

An important aspect for a business seller is attractiveness. The attractiveness relates to what the business looks like to outside potential buyers. Does the company run without the owner, is there a concentration of the customer base, does the company have high turnover, are they bringing new products or services to the market, and many other factors are taken into consideration. The more attractive, the higher the multiple which can take that wealth gap and multiple that by millions.

Another crucial factor and probably the most important of them all is readiness. Is the owner ready to sell the company or do they want to hold on to it?

Businesses like most everything in life are either growing or dying. If the owner is not ready to sell, they should be strategically and actively growing. There are many proven and evaluated fundamental strategies that can multiply the bottom and top line of a business. It takes about the same amount of effort that you normally exhaust, why not use the same time, and get that much more. You can outrun Mother Nature, but you will never beat Father Time. That is why if a business owner is either stale, tired or cannot hit that next level, it is important to bring in an expert to help kick start the growth. There are strategies, examples and stories in the following chapters that can accelerate your growth.

Why is readiness important? Because most business sales that have a contract to sell fall apart because the owner is not ready to sell. Primarily the owners are still emotionally attached and do not know what is next in their life and what they are going to do but that is a personal decision. In the meantime, you can prepare to maximize your business assets while you are still driving the ship and get the most out of your greatest asset.

What makes a business attractive to a buyer? An owner that can step away and the company still runs efficiently without them. These types of businesses command a higher multiple and supply the most amount of selling profits.

This book is designed to be more like a manual where you can reference ideas, thoughts, and strategies with a quick reference index in the back.

There are many ways to sell a business and many strategies. It is not one size fits all and in later chapters, we will dive into that.

Also, on the flip side, you can expand your business by making strategic acquisitions whether you just pick up their customers, assets, or distribution. This is a way to expand your business and make it attractive and worth more on a sale.

You can sell the business in many ways. The better systems that are in place combined with a highly polished presentation the bigger the return. There are ways that instead of you waiting for someone to knock on your door to buy your business, you can tap on theirs and they will come running with money falling out of their pockets to take your business over and to pay you. We will explore that in later chapters

I just wanted to lay a light foundation that if you only read these few pages, you can gain some valuable insight. Most books that are bought are never read. I want this one not just to be read but to be actionable.

For more information or get involved with us reach out to Jan Capital Inc. www.jancapitalinc.com

Chapter 5

GET THE MOST OUT OF YOUR BUSINESS

In this chapter, we'll look at ten mistakes hard-working business owners make that prevent them from making as much money as they can.

Before we get into the list of mistakes, let's think about the opportunity that we have previously discussed in earlier chapters that talk about how business owners are able to have success. If you don't have capital flowing in your business account, then you have a strategic plan on how the business can receive help from having cash on hand to operate business.

"There are two types of people who will tell you that you cannot make a difference in this world: those who are afraid to try and those who are afraid you will succeed." — Ray Goforth

Squeeze everything out of your business and that doesn't mean go out and take every dollar your business is worth and spend it but on other hand, find strategic ways to find every avenue to grow your business. Which is receiving every dollar your business is worth without missing any opportunities. For example, if you have 100 customers that buy your product, instead of constantly looking for new customers to sell to you, the business owner should focus on adding more products to those same 100 loyal customers. For starters, it gives you the opportunity to have consistent cash from your loyal customer because they're already committed to you, so therefore they're willing to support more of the items you have. Oftentimes, as business limits the company to only certain styles of product or only sale in certain regions is an example of not squeezing everything out of your business, which at times hinder companies from taking the next step. Last thing you want to do as a business owner is miss opportunities to sell or get money from a bank to get more inventory to sell.

There is a constant cycle in business, it's finding a way to create, and I often reiterate this because I understand how important it is because you get to stay in front of the market, which is the biggest benefit, but you also get more out of your particular business one would have expected. We often see companies grow nationally or even globally to a certain degree and we often think what's the difference between a smaller company in the same industry then a larger company and their clear differences financially but the one thing they both can offer is creativity and variety for its customer base.

Customers play a huge role in your business, in fact they are a part of your business, and the particularly small business must grow their relationship with their customers, which creating a wonderful experience and offering them the right product or services is a main step to get the most out of your business. It creates consistent cash flow, which allows you to use the money to get more money and continue to grow expeditiously. Use what you must create more, we often feel like we don't have enough but most times it takes for you to bring in all you have and create more avenues from there.

Mistake 1: Making Your Business Your Job, Not Your Investment

In today's ever-changing business environment, the longer you hold onto an asset, the greater chance of survival you have—whether it's real estate or precious metals. Even the stock market has proven that the longer you hold onto an asset (even when factoring in difficulties), the more the investment usually increases in value.

However, the longer you're in a business, the less chance of survival you'll have. There is no proof that the age of the company makes the company more profitable. For the average business, the longer you're in business, the less likely you'll be to make a profit year after year.

For instance, less than 44% of new companies make it past four years. Only 20% make it to ten years, and less than

10% make it to 20 years (which is truly disheartening). So, the more blood, sweat, and tears you put in, the less chance you have of surviving.

So How Do You Buck the Trend?

Treat your business as if you're an investor. Make sure you get a solid Return on Investment (ROI)—just like you'd expect to make money when you invest in the stock market or someone else's business. If you consider all your expenses, costs, and payments as investments, you'll see a return on your capital. For instance, you buy inventory and expect to make a profit. You expect to get a return on all cash going out the door, whether it's for payroll, marketing, or rent.

Not only does this tactic work *in* business, but it also works *for* your business. More will be explained below.

Mistake 2: Being Tactical but Not Strategic

It's easy to claim that your business decision-making is strategic, as far as getting your business to the next level. While you'll have a singular, focused strategy, you'll have numerous tactics. Once you have a strategy, you've decided in advance a goal you'd like to achieve for each tactic.

Meanwhile, your tactics apply to the day-to-day operations of your business. One example is an innovative marketing approach, such as a newsletter, a speaking engagement, a sales call, a trade show, a newspaper ad, or a meeting with a new client.

Before you deploy one of these tactics, you must decide the objective you'd like to achieve. For example, you're about to have an interaction with a customer (like a sales call), and your supervisor asks you what you want to achieve. Your reply would probably be simple: "To make a sale." But you should challenge yourself to achieve a lot more. Maybe you want to build a "disempowering message" about your competition. Or maybe you want to build a referral program or plant a seed that will generate more referrals. Or perhaps you want to arm all your customers with better information. Remember, every client you have is a potential salesperson for your organization.

Smart Operators #1

The owner of a hair salon noticed how high customer turnover was. This turnover was occurring for many reasons; customers weren't happy with the cut or the hairdresser, lack of time and they simply bounced around. But it was a relatively big salon, and they brought in about 150 clients a week.

So, Operators #12 wisely collected the customer's contact information and set up a three-email system. The first email involved regenerating the clients who do not come in that often: "Come back and get a half-price cut." The second email involved keeping in contact with the current customers: "Just a reminder that it's time to schedule your cut." The third email was a voucher for a referral: 50% off for the current customer's friend and 50% to the referrer on their next visit. With this system, Operators #12 doubled her business in five months.

This type of strategy is the fastest way to generate sales. The larger the inactive customer base, the larger the return. As you can see from this example, the process is easy. If you follow your email with a call, your results will quadruple.

Also, keep contact with your current customer base. Always go for referrals. So many businesses are built on referrals, and they don't even have a formalized referral system in place. Use this dumb luck to your advantage. Don't just set up one referral system, but several.

Referrals are the best type of customer. Since they already trust you, they'll usually buy right away and purchase more.

What do you want your client to say? How will you achieve this goal? If you're not thinking everything through (i.e., strategizing), your tactics won't maximize the opportunity at hand.

Once you set your expectations for each tactic, you need to create an actual policy or procedure that will effectively implement your idea on a tactical level. Also, your tactics should work together to achieve the outcome you want.

Most companies do not look at their tactics as an integrated program. For example, let's say you put all your best potential buyers in the same room at the same time. Would your sales message be consistent, or would it be unique to each customer? But if you had one single opportunity to pitch something to them all simultaneously, you could change your life forever—if you properly execute it. Or you could ruin your life if you're ineffective.

So, while tactics are the normal day-to-day functions of your business, the strategies guide them and take your business to a higher level. While answering the phone, doing accounts payable, and paying the delivery driver are necessary to keep the business running, they're not creating your long-term stability and a bright future.

Employing effective strategies could involve cutting the costs of your product. Or they could mean going through your customer list, reaching out to former customers and converting them back into current customers. Other examples of effective strategies include moving our business or creating a joint venture that allows you to cross-utilize your customer base and double your sales.

How Do You Become Strategic, Rather Than Merely Tactical?

Is everyone associated with your business performing the everyday tactics? Is anyone working to make the business better? If not, your business could fall into a shrinking lifecycle. If you spend all your time doing day-to-day tactics, you need to fire yourself and rehire yourself (with some help) to develop a strategy that will grow your business and significantly increase your bottom line. Then the money you spend on day-to-day tactics will be a great investment for the long-term success and profitability of your business.

Mistake 3: Not Understanding the Fundamentals of Business

It is important to know and understand the fundamentals of any business. Unfortunately, they don't teach you this in school or during on-the-job training. In fact, 99% of all business owners have never been exposed to the blueprint of an effective business.

My degree from the "school of hard knocks" cost hundreds of thousands of dollars, but I finally learned. However, once you learn, you can develop a true blueprint for long-term success. This lesson involves breaking the larger categories down into segments of your business. Then, you can concentrate on these segments and make improvements to each as needed.

There are only seven ways to grow a business. There might be hundreds of tactics, but you only need to understand the following seven categories of strategies to maximize your business:

1. Get more customers. This strategy is the most expensive one. It involves the following tactics:

   a. Referral systems. With these, you can either get clients and break even upfront, or you can make a profit on the backend.

   b. Guarantee buys through risk-reversal.

   c. Joint venture relationships.

   d. Use direct mail, email, and other forms of communication.

   e. Use telemarketing.

   f. Run extraordinary events or information nights.

   g. Buy qualified lists.

2. The second way is to get your customers to buy more often. This can be done via specials, promotions, and refills. You can also use the following tactics:

   a. Develop a consistent selling message.

b.   Increase the perceived value of your product/service through better customer education.

c.   Utilize public relations.

d.   Enhance the sales skills of your staff.

e.   Qualify leads upfront.

f.   Make irresistible offers.

g.   Give your clients reasons to buy via educating them.

h.   Deliver better than expected service.

i.   Frequent communication.

3.   The third way is to make your average transaction price higher: "Would you like a drink with your order?" It's relatively easy to get customers to buy a bundle when they are ordering. For instance, you can easily get them to buy an add-on product or service. Here are other ways to upsell your clients:

a.   Develop a backend of products that you can offer them.

b.   Maintain positive relationships with them by personally communicating with them (via phone, text, email, letter, etc.).

c.   Endorse other people's products.

d.   Run extraordinary events (such as "closed door sales" and limited prereleases).

e.   Pre-frame or program clients.

f.   Utilize price inducements.

4. A longer-term way involves adding a new product or service every year, to help build your sales funnel. Regardless of the type of business you're in, it's possible to periodically add a product or service to your offerings.

5. Since a joint venture cross-utilizes someone else's customer base, it's mutually beneficial. Here's the first question to ask: "Other than you, who has the most to gain from you being successful?" For example, a lawn guy develops trust with a customer by offering to recommend a discount on her carpet cleaning. Or a restaurant gets with a business whose employees have a limited lunch breaks because it's inconvenient for them to leave the office.

6. Another strategy involves buying out the competitor, which can be conducted via the following tactics:

   a.   You could buy outright and pick up their customer base—if they haven't really created a company but are functioning like a self-proprietor.

   b.   You could offer more money now with fewer headaches. For instance, they wouldn't have the added overhead, and they could get paid by you. They could go do something else and make added money. The advantage to you is that you cut a competitor and pick up a customer base that you could mine. You could also expand the product offering by following the first three ways to grow a business.

7. Or you just get lucky.

How to Read the Blueprint

If you're banking on getting lucky, it's just a matter of time until your fortune changes, or you hit a bump in the road. Once you understand that all businesses fit into these seven blueprints, you must focus on the first three. If you employ these tactics and strategies, you will grow your business and increase your profits.

You only need to concentrate on one at a time. Add a tactic in with strategic focus. Once you do that, add another tactic, and watch how you multiply your business in a brief period. If you quickly employ the strategy into the category with tactics, your profits will double, triple or more.

Mistake 4: Not Using Referrals

Most businesses don't realize that their current customer base is their best salesforce. They take it for granted that their customers might refer other customers, which they can only do by word of mouth. So, they do not formalize a referral system or (better yet) multiple referral systems. Your current customer base already trusts you and buys from you; when they refer others to you, the credibility is outstanding.

Have Formalized Referral Systems

Some business owners hesitate to ask for referrals because they somehow feel it is "inappropriate." They fear that customers will see it as overstepping their boundaries by getting too personal.

Think about the amount of business you currently get through referrals when you're not even trying. Now imagine getting five, ten, or even twenty times that amount. That's the potential of a formal referral system.

The best part is that a customer referral program will bring you immediate results: your customers and profits will start growing as soon as you put the system in place—since referral customers are like your best current clients. A referral-generated customer will normally spend more money and buy more often. They're almost always the most profitable, loyal, and likable part of your customer base.

So, there's no reason to be embarrassed, timid, or unduly sensitive about asking your customers or clients to direct other customers to you. Remember that most of your customers, clients, or patients really do have a relationship with you. They trust your company. They appreciate the product or service you provide.

Here are some effective, workable techniques for securing referrals:

- Write satisfied customers a letter telling them you're about to make a major marketing effort for new clients. But before you go to the mass market, you'd like them to have the first chance at telling their friends or associates.

- Offer inducements to customers for bringing in referrals.

- Offer a special incentive for their friends on their first purchases.

- Offer to perform a free service or consultation for any referral prospect.

- Give a clinic, seminar, or training session to your customers, and tell them they can invite one or two guests.

- Give your customers a free service for one month or quarter if they successfully refer someone to you. That way, your customer gets the credit. Make sure the prospect they recommend is qualified.

Mistake 5: Ignoring Your Finances

You don't have to be a CPA to have a good key understanding of financial statements. To succeed, it's critical that you understand your financial position, what your business generates for your product and/or service, and how that relates to your profit. For instance, you could have a product line that brings in 80% of your sales, but only makes 1% of your profit.

Break Your Financial Situation Down

You don't have to be a financial wizard. If you

can balance a checkbook, you can understand your financial position. To analyze your financial situation, you must break down each product or segment. You'll then know where your profit comes from, and what it takes to get that profit.

It's also critical to know how you spend your money and how you're paying for your expenses. In my experience, every business that analyzes their expenses gets an immediate 10% increase in their profits, just by understanding how much cash is going out and adjusting for it. The more you currently ignore your financial situation (whether it's good or bad), the more significantly you can improve your financial future by paying more attention to it.

Perhaps your financial situation is bad, and you're ignoring it. If so, you can take corrective action. But if you're checking the situation, you could adjust, increasing your odds of staying in business.

Mistake 6: Not Having a Consistent Selling Message

If you ask a company why they're better than their competitors, most of them will tell you they have superior quality, price, and service. But this answer is generic, and it has no meaning for your customers. Most small business owners don't employ a consistent marketing message. They just hop on bandwagons without giving a clear, consistent message in the market. Their message doesn't offer anything unique that will make them stand out from the crowd. It's just a message: "Buy from us." But it doesn't really offer a call to action.

So, it's no surprise that most businesses lacking a consistent sales message are barely able to get by. Their failure rate is high, their owners aren't interested, and they don't understand the importance of consistent messaging. They only get a small share of the potential business. Maybe they're in a fantastic location. But if they weren't, there wouldn't be any reason to buy from them. They lack a compelling promise, a standout feature, or a special service.

Would you want to buy from a small business that's just "there"? That lacks a unique benefit, doesn't have great price, a large number of choices, or an inviting storefront or guarantee? Or would you prefer to buy from a small business that offers a broad choice? Or maybe you'd choose a business that's half the price of competitors? Or that offers the finest products in your industry?

Smart Operators #2

The owner of a driveway-sealer company was making an average amount of money until he changed his strategy. He sent an email out to his old customers: "It's time to reseal your driveway. And you can get a 20% discount!"

Then he developed a brochure called "Why Sealing Is Important and How My Techniques Are Better." He followed up by personally visiting each customer's house. When he visited, he'd educate the customer and show them why his service was better and explained that his process was more expensive. He increased the perceived value, so he could justify the price he charged his customers.

At the same time, he knew that the average driveway needed to be resealed every 2 to 4 years. So, he offered to hold the price they'd previously paid and he told them he'd inspect the driveway seal every six months. If anything needed to be touched up, he'd do it for free, if they gave him a 20% deposit on the future service.

Soon, he went from being a two-person operation doing $200k a year to a ten-person operation doing over $2 million and he was booked for the next few years.

Attack your customer list and get them to reorder. Educate the customer about why your service is better. You don't necessarily have to be better. Even if you offer the same service, the customer will perceive your process as being superior because you explained it to them personally. Your competitor can't just come back later and say, "That's what I do, too."

Create the opportunity to build sales in the future. If you never make an offer, they'll never accept one.

Get a Consistent Message to Build Your Business

So, you've decided to develop a consistent selling message (CSM). Perhaps your company offers the broadest selection of products or services. You say they're "instantly available" or "always in stock."

If so, make sure your statement is true! Maybe in reality, you only keep 6 out of 25 items in stock, and you only have a few of each item. If so, the essence of your CSM promise is false, which will probably cause your marketing to fail.

It's important to try to create the "big promise" for your CSM. If you don't really believe that you can deliver on your CSM, choose another choice to build the foundation for your business. Ensure that you can stand out from the crowd and that you can deliver on it!

The CSM is the foundation that gives your business the ability to build a consistent image, to achieve success, exposure, and money. So, it's important for you to clearly and concisely articulate your CSM. If you're unable to effectively articulate it, your market won't be able to understand it either. If a potential customer needs the type of product or service you offer, your CSM should easily convey this message and bring your company to the forefront.

By making the CSM clear and concise through marketing and performance, you'll enable your business to stand out. It's important to trim the CSM down to a concise statement. When saying the sales pitch, the reps should refer to the CSM with its features, benefits, and/or advantages. By maximizing your CSM, you can show your potential customers how your product or service is superior.

When a mature company creates a powerful, appealing, fresh CSM, it will breathe new life into your marketing strategy, and it will generate renewed interest and excitement. So, you can evolve and keep standing out, rather than being another weak company that takes advantage of potential customers and traps them into listening to a sales pitch. Remember, if you don't evolve, you'll never appeal to your customers, no matter how hard you try.

Most CSMs are designed to appeal to a niche segment of the market, instead of the whole. There's a big gap from the high-end clients and discount seekers. More than likely, you won't be able to reach both groups with the same CSM.

Here are some examples of concise messaging:

- "They'll fight over it when you're dead." (Saddleback leather)

- Nerd Fitness "Stop taking advice from the dark side. There's a better way to get healthy." (Nerd Fitness)

- "Loans that change lives." (Kiva)

And here are some examples of a CSM building a strong brand:

- "We're #2; we try harder." (Avis)

- "When it absolutely, positively has to be there overnight." (Fedex)

- "A diamond is forever." Debeers

You must create a CSM that can catch on as a slogan. You want your customers to associate it with you at once. You must also have a consistent story to go with your image.

Ask yourself these questions:

- What long-term reputation do you want?

- Are you operating today in a way consistent with that reputation?

- How do you want to be perceived?

- How do you do things better than everyone else?

Every company has something unique to offer—something that sets you apart. If you don't, then you should. So, you'd better take the time to communicate it.

So, What's Different About You?

In other words, what perception do you want the market to ultimately have about your products or services? Does your current marketing ultimately reflect your reputation and your long-term strategies?

To maximize your marketing effectiveness, you need to consider what you want to say. Think through all the questions people ask. You can build your story by piecing together the answers. You'll get most of these people to want to do business with you. The better your story is, the better your marketing will be.

Mistake 7: Not Understanding Your Biggest Asset

Your customer relationships are your greatest asset. You can secure these relationships by:

a. Keeping in touch

Whether you communicate via phone, text, email, mail, or in-person, all customers want to feel like they're special, and that you take a personal interest in their needs.

b. Providing post-purchase reassurance

Each time a customer places an order with you, communicate with them a week after they receive your product or service, and seek feedback. Customers appreciate that.

c. Giving your customers the best deals and guarantees possible.

d. Offering preferential pricing

Let your best and "oldest" customers in on the best deals first. Give them the opportunity to take advantage of specials and sales before the public has the opportunity.

e. Building rapport and trust

Be as honest as you can be with your customers. People want to buy from sellers they trust.

Keep a correct and timely customer list. Updating and reusing your customer list is crucial. If you have a solid customer list, you have a solid customer base. Work the customers you already have; they've bought from you before. If they had a valuable experience, they'll buy from you again. Even if you only have a moderate number of customers, at once initiate a perpetual communication with them, to show them that you're their trusted friend and advisor.

What Can You Do?

The first thing to do is communicate within five to seven days after your customer's first transaction. In this letter, do the following:

- Thank them.

- Resell the value of your company.

- Reassure them that buying your product or service was a wise move.

Before a major effort, it's always a clever idea to test your messages, because they'll differ in just about every situation. Also, consider offering your customers an added product or service they can purchase on a preferred basis. Or if the item they bought can be exchanged or returned, try to upsell a larger unit.

Reconnect With Former Customers

If you have a customer base, you have former customers. Go back to these customers and try to convert them from former to current customers. There are only a few reasons why they stopped buying:

- They no longer need the product.

- They moved out of the area.

- They had a terrible experience.

Each one of these customers can be brought back into the fold.

Mistake 8: Not Minimizing Debt

Should you borrow money? Not if you can get cash from your business. Most business owners think of getting cash and operating capital from outside sources. This tendency puts a lot of pressure on you as the owner—not only professional pressure to increase cash flow and pay off debts, but also personal pressure. You're responsible for the debt. As discussed earlier, make your expenditures create a return, not just an expense.

You can generate cash from your assets, namely your business. There are several ways to mine that asset. You can generate hundreds or even thousands of dollars if you work on your customer list or do a joint venture with another business. So, you should try these tactics before you borrow outside money.

Why go to a bank, a friend, or a relative when you might have ten times that amount lying dormant in your customer base? Utilize that money first! Mine every dime that exists in your own accounts before you start asking more.

It might even be faster to mine your business, instead of getting a loan from a bank. It might take you four weeks or longer to get a bank loan. In that same period, you can write a sales letter with a great offer, evaluate it with a group of a thousand customers, and follow up with them. Instead of trying to borrow $25,000 from the bank, you could have $100,000 in your treasury before the bank even says "yes" or "no." And that's all your money. You don't owe anyone anything.

You don't have to pledge your assets, your house, your mortgage, or anything else! The best part is that you didn't create another expenditure that doesn't return cash.

Smart Operators #3

Another smart operator was struggling with a medical-supply delivery service. In fact, he was just breaking even. So, he entered a joint venture with an auto-parts delivery business.

After his drivers dropped off the medical equipment, they'd pick up the auto parts and deliver them. They split the cost of the drivers, which made the medical company more profitable. And the auto parts store was selling more parts because they didn't have a delivery option before their joint venture began.

Who can help your business grow with kind products or services? How can you use 100% of your capacity?

Mistake 9: Not Understanding the Value of Your Customer

The value of a customer is defined as the marginal net worth and lifetime value of the customer. It's the total aggregate profit your business makes, over the lifetime of an average customer. It includes all residual sales, less all advertising, marketing, and all fulfillment expenses for products or services.

Let's say your average new customer brings you a profit of $75 on the first sale. He repurchases three more times that year, and the average reorder is $300. On each $300 reorder, you make a gross profit of $150, and the average patronage life is two years.

So, every new customer is worth $1,050 to you. I arrived at that amount by totaling the $75 first profit and the three purchases per year at $150. Then I multiplied that amount by the two years he stayed a customer. Each customer is worth $1,050, and it costs you $30 in marketing and advertising to bring them in. So, every $30 you spend is worth $1,050.

Overall, you'd be foolish not to increase your marketing effort and gain customers. In other words, spend everything you can to bring in a customer, if they cost you less than you earn.

Smart Operators #4

Even though a chiropractor cannot guarantee changes to health, he or she can guarantee that the patient will be satisfied. So, Operators #4 did a "No Risk Satisfaction Guarantee." If the patient didn't want to go through with the treatments after the first exam, he'd refund their money. He also lowered the cost of the first treatment, which allowed him to get more people in the door.

Within four years, he's never had a patient take advantage of the no-risk satisfaction guarantee.

Make it easy to do business with you. Lower the bar with risk reversals and know the marginal net worth of your target customer. After you reel them in, they'll spend much more money than you invested.

This information is critical because it will allow you to know how much you can spend on marketing to get a sale. To calculate your marginal net worth, ask these questions:

- How many customers do you have?

- How often do they buy?

- How much do they buy?

- What is the profit margin on their average sale?

- How long do they buy from you? Over what period?

Technical but Essential

This section is a little technical. But if you can muddle through it, the value and knowledge you gain will be immense.

To calculate the lifetime value of your customers, do the following:

1) Compute precisely what a customer costs you to obtain by dividing your current marketing budget by the number of customers it's producing.

2) Calculate the cost of a prospect the same way.

3) Compute the number of sales you get for so many prospects (i.e., the percentage of prospects that become your customers) and the cost of converting those prospects into customers.

4) Average the cost to generate a sale, and the cost to generate *and* convert a prospect. This amount is your average cost for at once producing a customer.

5) Subtract the amount determined above from your customer's average first purchase. This amount will give you your profit on his or her first purchase.

6) Compute your average repeat sale and your average profit on that sale.

7) Calculate how much added profit a customer is potentially worth to you over his or her lifetime of patronage by determining how many times most customers come back. Multiply that number by the average profit per repeat sale. Be conservative.

The big money is in repeat sales and ancillary sales. That's the "back end." It's one of the keys to successful marketing. Once someone buys from you, it's much easier to get them to buy again repeatedly. It's less expensive, too! You don't have to spend as much money on sales costs as you do on the front end.

Instead, you can resell, upsell, and cross-sell all your customers. Reselling involves simply selling a customer the same thing he or she bought before. Upselling is getting the customer to buy a better, more expensive, or more sophisticated product. Cross-selling is getting him or her to buy a complementary added product.

What are you selling on the back end right now? What could you be selling? How do these statistics affect the lifetime value of your average customer?

The easiest thing to do is upsell your customer. Many businesspeople don't upsell, but the ones who do often persuade 30-40% of their customers to buy added or more expensive products. They do it at the point of purchase by offering the customer either a larger unit or a joint package of other products or services that complements what they are already buying.

If 30-50% of your customers are upsold successfully, that's the easiest, fastest way to increase your average margin. Let's say that your normal unit of sale is $50, but you're able to put it "on special" for $30 because "you got a great buy on it." If so, you might make another $15 on that sale. You could further increase your profit on each sale by an added $3.75 for every four customers that come through the door.

Offer larger units, higher grades, and longer payment periods. Or add a larger package of products/services with a higher perceived value at a large discount for customers who buy right away. Or add a more prolonged service agreement. Do anything that will increase your profit per transaction.

How to Make This a Reality

I don't know about you, but I've saw many people who fail to achieve goals, simply because they don't know how to turn an abstract idea, concept, or objective into a tangible reality.

What inhibits or prohibits people from achieving their goals? Many things, and I believe all of those can be overcome if you truly wish to super-achieve and are willing to pay the necessary price in effort, perseverance, and action.

First, let's explore the primary reasons people do not accomplish a goal. The most common are inertia, fear of failure, lack of experiencing self-induced success, and habitual negative thinking.

Most people have kept their current mindsets for a long time. They simply cannot break out of their mental strangleholds, even if the desire exists. Like gravity, inertia holds people back from achieving their true potential.

How do you effectively break inertia's insidious grasp on your potential? Start by carrying out a series of small but meaningful successes outside the scope of your normal business operations. "Psych out" your subconscious disposition for negativity and skepticism, then replace it with a positive experience related to achievement. By using this approach, your mind will start believing you can achieve things.

Start Small and Take Baby Steps

Try sending a special promotion to a few of your customers or prospects. It could be a special upsell package or an addon approach at the point of sale. Or contact a certain number of (e.g., 50, or 100, or 500) old prospects or inactive customers via phone, email, letter, or in-person visit and make them an irresistible sales offer. Or go to another company and propose a joint venture for an endorsement test or cross-utilization of customer lists.

All these options are designed to compel you to get into the habit of acting, then seeing your actions pay off. They teach your mind that it can try new things. These options are also designed to confirm the notion that these fundamental business strategies really do work. They will pay off for you if you put them into action by taking a few small steps. By visibly seeing their success in your own business or practice, you'll condition yourself to progress to more expansive, lucrative accomplishments.

First, find the most viable and adaptable concepts. Then take some time to evaluate which one has the potential to produce the fastest or most profitable results. Next, concentrate on this concept until you either confirm or invalidate its applicability to your business.

Only try out only one solid promotional idea or marketing approach at a time. Thoroughly consider it. Then oversee and administer the implementation of the concept. Make sure you don't allow anyone to mismanage it.

Assuming the idea pays off, what do you do next? Don't abandon it! Before you move on to assessing another business-building idea, make sure you've taken steps to integrate the idea that you just validated as a perpetual part of your ongoing operations. The secret to enduring growth is perpetuating a proven concept, then adding a layer. Consider every marketing concept and figure out how to continuously profit from it (or derivatives of it).

Don't just use a concept once, forget about it, and move onto something new. Once you've proven something works, use it repeatedly, and whenever possible. Monitor its performance until you know for certain that it's no longer working. Don't ever drop winning concepts. Always expand them before pursuing something new. That's how you'll make your business grow and build solid, enduring layers of marketing profits. That's how you'll make your business grow.

Mistake 10: Not Having an Exit Strategy

Most people go into business because they believe they have a superior product or service. They have a burning passion, but they haven't defined their plan to leave. They have a delusional perspective that they're going to sell their business "someday" for a lot of money. Then they'll be able to travel the earth and have financial freedom, but they have no clue how. They don't understand who's going to buy it. They don't really try to maximize the sales price. They don't set the enterprise up to run itself.

Most business owners don't understand that if there are 3,000,000 businesses for sale through business brokers, only one in five is going to ever sell.

The market for exit strategies is very inefficient. Buyers and sellers can't find each other. When an entrepreneur is ready to sell in a week or two, there's no way to position their assets for maximum sales appeal. There's no long-term, fully developed plan to leave. When you realize how many business owners think they're building wealth when they're not, it's terrifying. Most entrepreneurs tend to think enthusiastically: "What can I do right now?" But it's necessary for them to start thinking longer-term, so they have clear perspectives and keep growing the asset value of their businesses.

Most people don't capitalize on downtimes and setbacks. Most businesspeople don't handle these times proactively.

So, if you do, you'll have a substantive advantage over your competitors who don't.

Always create an exit strategy and keep developing it.

For more information or get involved with us reach out to Jan Capital Inc. www.jancapitalinc.com

Chapter 6

THE RISK AND THE BIG REWARD

HOW TO ELIMINATE OR SHIFT RISK AND KEEP CONTROL

"Successful people do what unsuccessful people are not willing to do. Don't wish it were easier; wish you were better." — Jim Rohn

Overview – This area is important because risk is the foundation of all decisions, whether business or personal. Too much risk and you are out of business and too insignificant risk, you will spin your wheels and go nowhere. You need a balance.

Taking risks is part of the small business owner's life. What a small business owner must do is understand the risk and maximize the risk versus reward. If you spend all your time on your business and you're not making any real money, then it isn't worth it. The main point of being in business is to make money, and that solution will keep you in business for a long time. If one is not making money or taking the risk to eventually bring the money in, then they won't be in business for long, and it's that simple. I often personally interview different successful business owners and even professional athletes like myself and the one common thing they all did was take risks. Either it was from investing time and energy into their craft or business owners waking up every day to find unusual ways in the market to break through to success.

The risk before the reward is a real thing and finding what risk that you need to take to break through to success is important. Once you find what type of risk gets your business the big reward, you will enjoy it because you understand that's what it takes to continue to break through the barriers. By any means, it's not easy but the wonderful thing is, it's possible. As stated before, I converse with many diverse types of successful people from various types of industry and when you understand that it's all about finding out what works for you and sticking to it. The continuous effort to accomplish your goals despite the adversity is a part of the risk. The biggest regret that many of them mention that are successful is they should have taken risk earlier in their career, especially business owners. There is no reason to wait, if you have a business or are inspired to have one, take the risk that is required to get to where you need to be. Absolutely no shame in failing because one you will learn how to succeed through failure but also during the process learn what works.

TYPES OF RISK

Risk comes in many forms, but most small business owners only think of it as financial. However, the risk is relational, functional, opportunistic, and actionable as well. Financials are self-explanatory. The relational risk has to do with relationships, which could be with customers, employees, vendors, or anyone else that a business relationship can be formed with. In today's world, saying the wrong thing can bring a company down in a brief period of time.

An example of relational risk is when Coke introduced the New Coke. Their sales went way down, and they had to go back to the old Coke formula, and the New Coke was quickly discontinued. The risk was with their loyal customer base when they told them, "Hey! You don't know what is good, so we changed it and gave you the best". But the customers knew what they wanted – the original Coke and nothing else. The company risked their entire business by making this change. Fortunately for them, they were able to survive and go back to the original formula, and in time, became financially stable once more.

There are several types of employee risk. Promoting a bad employee to the position of a manager could cause you to lose a lot of good employees. Having an incompetent employee in charge of crucial business aspects could cause havoc. Similarly, when you have customer service personnel that hate people, this is never a good thing for your business. Another issue is when you hire and promote people for their looks or personality instead of merit.

There is also vendor risk. You rely on vendors to supply your quality product at a fair price. What if you beat your vendors up so much on the price and force them to go to a competitor to sell the product for more money? You'd also be at risk of losing your customers since the vendors can tell them who your customers are. Another issue is when a vendor provides an inferior or low-quality product, and you fail to realize until it's too late. This can make you lose valuable customers.

OPPORVENT

Opportunity risk is another type of risk. The ability to recognize this risk and act could make the company a significant profit or save it from massive losses.

OPPORVENT is when you seek the opportunity and combine it with inventing. Most people think of inventing as creating a new product. However, inventing is about turning an idea into a product or service. Most inventors spend their lifetime looking for the next important thing or an idea so great that everyone will pay them enough to retire. That is pure fantasy. Inventing is being able to take something, whether it is a situation, product, or opportunity and make something new from it. One smart operator had a company that sold a massager. There are millions of massagers on the market. However, they realized there was a gap in the market because massagers help with circulation. And who has low circulation? Older people and diabetics often have circulation issues.

Recognizing this factor, they created an average website and added videos and testimonials. They even made a nice flier explaining the benefits and showed how much healthier and happier the users were. Then they asked the most important question to take their invention to the next level, "who has relationships with the customers they want to reach?" Undoubtedly, doctors, medical professionals, and such! They targeted one segment at a time and went to the doctors. They put a unit for patients to use in the waiting room. No, they didn't try to sell to the doctor first. They wanted to prove the concept first. Eventually, the patients wanted to buy them for home use. They set the doctor up as a dealer and paid them $100 per sale. They then took the doctor's story, a testimonial, and went to other doctors and signed them up as dealers.

Bottom line: in under a year, they are selling over 2,000 units just in a small geographic area. That is where opportunity and inventing combine! There are so many ways and avenues to make money.

Risk comes in many forms; it is on the owner's shoulders to minimize it as much as possible.

COMPANY RISK EXAMPLES

In 1977, the senior administrators at Twentieth Century Fox made a decision that changed the eventual fate of their funds. They signed overall marketing rights for all Star Wars films in return for a token $20,000 cut in Lucas' studio paycheck. Twentieth Century Fox lost out on over **three billion dollars** of revenue by not realizing the value of the future earnings. They missed out on the biggest licensing deal in US history.

They surrendered all their rights to marketing Star Wars products for a measly $20k. Their risk was not upfront but rather was on the backend. They gave their rights and billions of dollars of revenue away! How much do you think that $20k is to an organization of that size? To them, it was pennies, yet the person who made the decision ought to have been shot. Their risk was the potential future risk. Those earnings would have grown the company and helped them achieve so much more. Perhaps, the organization could have gained a more solid footing.

The Beatles auditioned in 1962 with Decca Records. The official at Decca Records rejected them: he thought they sounded like a then known group called 'The Shadows', which never added up to anything. The Decca Records executive told the Beatles manager, "We don't care for your young man's sound. All the male groups are not popular, and small groups with guitars will never make money." Since then, more than two billion Beatles records have been sold around the world. The Beatles performed together for ten years, and if they hadn't broken up, they could have made even more.

This apparently was a poor choice and that is easy to say in hindsight. However, let's take a closer look at the situation. The Beatles were not approaching them for upfront cash but to hire them as a marketing and promotion company. Decca Records had no risk in the arrangement. Rather than taking them and evaluating them to see if they were profitable, they declined the offer even though they could have given them a trial and if things didn't work out, they could easily have gotten out of the agreement. This is a procedure utilized by numerous infomercial organizations today. They see an item that "may" have a future and they lock it up with the owner. No risk on their part, just future payments if the product is successful. Once they get the product locked up, they go around and get other people or companies to fund it. If they can't do this, they will scrap it. The product owner gets the product locked up and can't do anything with it and makes no money. The owner is the one that gets screwed on this deal. Therefore, it is important to have them put some "skin in the game" and pay money up front. If they don't put any cash upfront on the deal, then it means they have no confidence that the product will sell. Don't deal with them, they are not the right company for you.

In 1876, William Orton was the President of Western Union and had a business proposition for the biggest innovation at the time – the telephone. Bell offered to license the patent for the phone to Orton. Bell was asking for $100,000 in 1876 money, which is worth about two million dollars today. Orton considered the entire idea crazy, and composed a letter to Alexander Graham Bell, saying, "After careful thought of your innovation, while it is an exceptionally intriguing curiosity, we have arrived at the end that it has no business potential. What utilization could this organization make of an electrical toy?" After two years, the phone started to take off, Orton understood the greatness of his oversight, and put in years (unsuccessfully) to get Bell's licenses.

At that time, Orton was worth millions. The risk for him could have been substantial at 2 million dollars, but he could have minimized it. He did not recognize a revolutionary communication changing trend. Even today, certain products or concepts change the world, but you must recognize them. He could have used his power and done this deal with little to no risk on his part. He was well respected and well known in the industry, he failed on a few fronts. First, he should have analyzed and gotten more feedback from others. Second, he could have brought other people in as investors and controlled the deal with no risk.

The Eastman Kodak organization built a digital camera in 1975. At that point, they decided to sit on it and not take it to market because they thought it would hurt their film business. At this time, they had 90% of the US film market for cameras. In the mid-'80s, Fuji entered the US film commercial market with film and supplies. However, Kodak's administration thought that US shoppers would never relinquish their homegrown image. In the 1984 Olympics, Kodak had the chance to be the lead sponsor for film companies. Fuji won the rights instead. This gave Fuji a solid footing in the US market and catapulted them to US consumers. Kodak never was able to regroup and recover from their bad decisions and later filed for bankruptcy.

Kodak was "too big for their britches". This superiority complex drove them to make unwise decisions and assume that they would always dominate the market. They failed to minimize their risk by ignoring the competition. They should have attacked them at the very beginning. Instead, they opened the door and let the competition build a strong business and eventually devastate them in the market.

When the ET movie was launching in 1981, Amblin Productions asked Mars Company to do some cross-marketing. They asked if they could show M&Ms in the film, giving them the exposure in the movie. In return, they wanted Mars Company to advertise the movie on the backs of the candy bags. Mars declined the offer. Reese's Pieces, the not so notable M&M competitor, saw sales jump 65% in the months after the film highlighting their product. This was a springboard for future sales.

Mars Company had no risk in this deal. It would have cost them virtually nothing to print some promotions on their bags. Instead, they said no. This helped expand a competitor. If you can do a venture for free or low-cost advertising with zero risks, do it! If it won't hurt your brand, unlike a hot dog seller partnering with porn films, why not take advantage of it?

Gerald Levin: In 2000, he was the head of Time Warner. He was so confident in the purchase of America Online, he decided against hedging the bet by putting a collar on the transaction. A collar empowers the buyer—for this situation Time Warner—to return to the terms of the exchange if the purchaser's stock falls beneath a specific cost. When the merger was declared, and before it was finished, the Internet bubble burst and AOL shares halved in value. Without a collar in the contract, Time Warner didn't have the ability to renegotiate the purchase; this is usually standard language in a public company's stock purchase. Time Warner executives asked Levin to reevaluate the arrangement. Levin decided not to. The rest is history. Time Warner investors are still paying for his lack of risk management.

It was zero risk to include a clause in the contract to cover this. Instead, they received poor advice and considered the possible downsides of the transaction. The downside risk was obvious; they were buying a company at a certain stock price. What if the stock price moves or even goes to zero?

Greed blinded them to this possibility, as is common during a bubble.

A long way from its underlying foundations as a little Seattle Coffee shop, today Starbucks is the home of would-be writers and screenwriters all over the world and many other coffee enthusiasts. It's fitting those three scholars established this coffeehouse: an essayist (Jerry Baldwin), an English educator (Gordon Bowker) and a history instructor (Zev Siegl). They each put up $1,350 to start the business. 15,000 stores later, that small amount of risk has paid huge dividends.

$1,350 is generally safe for the upside; the only risk was they could have lost $1,350, which is not that much money.

In the past, Maglite was regarded as the world's best flashlight. Today, it has competition from LED and even iPhones. It is still known for consistent quality in an industry that emphasizes reliability over extravagance. It's well-known gear for police officers and military personnel. The organization's story starts when they set aside $125 and MagLite organizer, Tony Maglica, put his extended periods of working for other individuals behind him. With just a touch of capital and a machine shop, Maglica figured out how to manufacture an item that would turn into a powerhouse for battery electric flashlights.

He had the expertise to make a unit, and it cost him virtually nothing. With this minimal risk, he grew a big company and never had to work for anyone else again.

In 1923, the largest playground in the world was operating out of a garage at Robert Disney's home. At the time, the organization was called Disney Brothers studio and was situated close to the present Disneyland Park in Anaheim, California. In this one car garage, Disney and his partners were developing the Alice Comedies, which later became the basis for Alice in Wonderland. A brief time after that, Roy and Walt got a bigger space down the street and entered a joint venture with Universal Studios for a distribution agreement for the Alice Comedies.

They launched from this point and never looked back. They took small steps first with small risk and slowly expanded and built a world dominating company that employs over 75,000 people and is a leader in several market categories.

In 1945, before Mattel turned into a famous American toy producer, originators Matson, Ruth, and Elliot were making picture outlines out of a Southern California garage. They were making dollhouses and bringing them to a moderately successful relative that owned a furniture store. With the success of the dollhouses, Ruth thought of what else she could add to expand the product offering. She had a daughter whose name was Barbara, and she came up with the idea for Barbie dolls.

These powerhouse organizations were not the only ones that started small, with small upfront capital, Cloud, Box.net, Square and Tesla Motors all have one thing in common: starting in a small garage. A small space like a garage is not the only limited space many companies began, Nike began out of the trunk of a car, and Dell computers began out of a dorm room.

These are extreme examples, but you get the point. You must weigh the risk versus the reward and know what your tolerance level is, whether it be financial or emotional. If you can't afford to lose hundreds of thousands of dollars, don't put yourself in that situation; if you can't afford to lose $100, don't do that either. If you can't mentally handle it, find something else you are comfortable doing. Not everyone is cut out to be a business owner, and that is ok. If you have ever heard the song from the 70's group BTO "If you ever get annoyed, look at me I'm self-employed, I love to work at nothing all day." Many times, which is the way of the small business owner, and it takes the understanding to make a shift, and that is OK. You need to do what is best for you and your family. Many times, people get caught in the emotion and lose focus on the goal which is usually to make as much money as possible in the shortest amount of time. Sometimes, working for someone else can make you more money than working for yourself. There are many ways to leverage what you have with minimal risk. This is discussed in later chapters.

HOW CAN YOU DEFINE RISK AND SEIZE THE OPPORTUNITY?

Understanding your business's risk profile helps you make a realistic risk assessment. This takes a small amount of effort and time but can save you millions of dollars.

- Define risk limits

- Calculate risk resistance, both fiscally and otherwise

- Evaluate risk before making any major or move

- Make risk-reward tradeoffs in day-by-day administration

- Attack apparent and genuine dangers

Plainly characterize risk resistance and prepare strategies. This will help insure the business against seeking single, restricted objectives without considering potential results while deciding the "proper" level of risk. What is proper and worthy for one individual or business might be unsuitable for another.

RISK RESILIENCE

Risk resilience is the businesses or people's apparent tolerance for potential misfortune or misfortunes. For instance, numerous individuals who risk their money gambling weigh the potential loss of money versus the possible gain. Businesses will allocate an extensive variety of risks among various parts of the organization. While risk resilience summaries are supposed to give direction, chance mentalities mirror a more extensive theory and approach. This is resolved and driven by the basic culture, convictions and aggregate level of the people inside the association. Risk tolerance varies among singular administrators, business owners, and individuals.

You may have an extreme hunger for producing millions of dollars inside your portfolio. However, by and large, there is a cutoff on what you can endure. What is a primary driver of tolerance? Your paycheck, housing costs, educational cost and expenses are a few. How these factors affect your risk management in accomplishing the multi-million-dollar target play into your own risk resilience. This isn't quite the same as an organizational stance. Individuals and organizations could have polarizing risk assessments; that's why when weighing the risk versus the rewards, it's important to calculate the risk to the individual or organization. A large organization might make a relatively small, calculated risk of

$500k but an individual might find that that amount could bankrupt them or vice versa.

Characterizing limits: The craziness of the late 2000's contained numerous examples of associations that either purposely or accidentally took on a lot of risk in the quest for financial gains. These companies risked bankruptcy and paid serious financial penalties. Looking back, a considerable number of these companies had not set satisfactory limits nor characterized, verbalized, conveyed and implemented a solid risk management strategy. Companies that defined their risk tolerance either did not partake or had exit strategies and hedges for their companies. They did not suffer the consequences of giving out free money that destroyed many companies and decimated an entire industry.

You should take chances that the company or organization can assess in advance. Compare risk and reward, against the effect and cost of overseeing the dangers for the organization. Acknowledge potential loss of x% of dollars for a half likelihood of expanding sales by x%. Risk resistance proclamations are worthless if they are not comprehended and incorporated into choices of the day-by-day administration. The objective is to build up a culture where all representatives understand and are utilizing risk and reward. You may have, "the business has zero hunger (or resistance) for movement" or "the business has zero resilience for blackouts past x time in span." Integrated into day-to-day administration, this may result in a boss terminating an employee for unscrupulous behavior, regardless of whether the actions brought about a 1 dollar or a 1-million-dollar misfortune or changing business procedures and future approaches to deal with all business transactions.

Comprehending and characterizing risk resistance is essential for an organization's risk analysis strategy. Management's understanding of risk, and how complex their plans are for accomplishing targets, is important to the general wellbeing and practicality of the organization. The test in employing a powerful risk management strategy is in adjusting the risk/reward calculation in comparison to the long-term economic result and to ensure the organization not only survives but thrives.

All responsibility falls solely on the owner. It's not the employees that will lose everything, they can simply just move to another employer that might pay them more. The owner could pay an immense price not only in their financial security but also their families, and in the freedom to do the things they want on their preferred schedule.

Reducing all risks in business is difficult. If the risk is too low or never tested operationally, the potential for reward will probably be low (except if it is a specialty market or restricted, controlled business model). If the risk is too high or not understood by the decision makers and their representatives, it can have extraordinary negative outcomes for the business.

Monetary outcomes are the most widely recognized and easiest evaluated segments in risk assessment. Monetary outcomes and measurements are an essential part of risk tolerance. However, risk resistance and tolerance should be evaluated past monetary execution norms. Risk drives both positive and negative outcomes. In this manner, risk resilience should not be assessed with a purely negative focus, but also with an eye to the possible upsides.

One smart operator bought a company that sold a retail product in the trade show market. When he bought the company, it did around 100 shows per year, and the owner would brag about how they never had a show that lost money. After purchasing the company, the smart Operators understood risk and reward. He immediately went and did over 400 shows per year, with only 20 losing money and quadrupling the bottom line. The former owner was risk averse and over the years, left millions of dollars on the table and never knew it.

HOW CAN YOU MINIMIZE THE RISK?

Before making important decisions, you should ask the following:

1. What is my objective?

2. How much is this going to cost financially?

3. How much is this going to cost emotionally?

4. How much time is this going to suck up?

5. What's the best possible outcome?

6. What's the worst thing that could happen?

7. What else could go wrong?

8. Could this place me in a stranglehold?

9. Are the owner and staff disciplined enough to ensure that it will happen?

10. Am I willing to do what it takes to get through this?

Always weigh your risk/reward in your business functions and strategy. It could be as simple as launching a new product line or having competent customer service personnel. Side note: rule one in customer service is to hire people that like people, you would be surprised how many small business owners' customer service people, the face of the company, don't like people. Other things to consider are hiring, spending too much without getting a return, rent, salaries, sales, expenses, and so on.

ELIMINATE STICKY FINGERS AND KEEP YOUR HARD-EARNED CASH

What is the risk of employees managing all your financial transactions? Potentially huge, control your cash and never give anyone the ability to clean you out.

One of the biggest risks facing small business owners is employee theft and it is devastating to companies. Thieves are clever and can find ways to steal from the owners without their knowledge. It costs US small businesses over $40 billion dollars a year.

One employee set up an elaborate system where he established a website in his name, took the order for a product, had the company ship the product, and then collected the money. Because of his position with the company and his perceived trustworthiness, he was able to pocket thousands of dollars before he was caught. This caused the owner to change the company procedures and controls, but it was too late to avoid taking a monetary hit.

One unscrupulous employee pirated the company's Amazon account, changing it to his own. All the payments coming from sales were shifted to the thief's personal account. In addition, the thief started a side business and had other employees perform services without the owners' knowledge. The owner eventually found out and pressed charges.

He isn't alone in having bad employees. An independent study uncovered that the typical theft from a small business averaged a $1.13 million loss. Small companies are hit by this loss 68% of the time. The average loss for small businesses was $289,864. Unfortunately, the theft usually goes unnoticed for a lengthy period and is devastating to the small business. Usually, the embezzlers are trusted employees of the company and many times, they are very senior staff members.

The most common theft is embezzlement, about one-third of all cases are this type. Check fraud makes up about 22.1%. 70% of check fraud usually occurs in a small business with less than 100 employees. Surprisingly, most small business owners view vandalism as a bigger threat than embezzlement.

The highest financial losses are generally small dollar amounts over an extended period. This is less noticeable and harder to detect than losing a large sum of money in a brief period. Many of these schemes have lasted over 5 years. Most small business owners believe embezzlement and employee theft is one big hit and they are done. When tiny amounts are taken over an extended period, the average loss over 5 years is $2.2 million, for ones that go over ten years, it's $5.4 million.

HOW TO PREVENT THEFT

Institute checks and balances, never let one person have end-to-end control of cash. If the employee is a check signer, do not allow them to print the checks. Smaller businesses should have the bank statements sent straight to the owner's home from the bank. The owner can review and ensure that there are no suspicious transactions. The owner needs to understand the payments, the vendors, and the normal flow of the payment system to reduce fraud. It is their money, and they need to take responsibility for it. If these steps are not taken, that gives employees the opportunity to cover up the fraud through manipulating the company's books.

What type of employee is stealing? The average age for the embezzlers is 48 years old for women and 49 years old for men. 56% are women. Embezzlers act like good employees; diligent and always ready to work, early and out late, never take a vacation. Often, there are hints in the employees' behavior. Thieves usually will make high-ticket purchases that a normal person making that salary couldn't afford. There are many stories that the employees will tell to hide their theft, including pulling up in their new car with a story about buying and selling cars. Sometimes it is hard to distinguish these employees from others because they have the same traits as a good employee; you would too if you were making two or three times more than you could make anywhere else.

Most frauds are uncovered when the thieving employee is on vacation. Most small business owners never recover their money.

HOW TO TELL IF YOU ARE BEING TAKEN TO THE CLEANERS

Most thieves have common traits - living above their means, financial problems, close relationships with suppliers, and want to control certain aspects of the business functions. If you pay attention, you can possibly detect and prevent theft.

Look for these warning signs to prevent theft, fraud or embezzlement:

- They refuse to take a vacation

- They frequently work overtime

- They take work home

- They spend excessively (new cars, trips) when their income couldn't support that

- Petty cash missing or turning over frequently

- High dollar expenses on employee travel

- They have a tight relationship with suppliers.

- Frequently have lunch with suppliers that are independent

- Sudden cash – Purchase for luxury goods when no raise was given, and they didn't hit the lottery.

- Keep tight control of the books – minor discrepancies in cash might appear minor, if large or frequent it could signal a problem

- Constantly missing items – not only small items like pens but other items such as electronics, tools and other items that could be easily sold can indicate theft

- Inventory shrinkage beyond normal levels of shoplifting

HOW DOES THE CASH STICK TO THEM

If you are aware of the warning signs, it can help you focus on where and how the problem is occurring and give you the opportunity to correct it. You need to develop internal controls to monitor theft and embezzlement:

- Deposit cash and checks daily and reconcile all accounts at least monthly. Never leave cash lying around, cash is king and is tempting for some thieves.

- Ensure independent financial functions of employees, the employee that writes checks should never be the one reconciling the bank statement.

- Monitor petty cash, require all transactions have a slip, receipt, or log, and require two signatures on the checks to replenish petty cash.

- Walk around the office, warehouse or factory and show employees you know what is going on in the company, out of sight out of mind. Be careful not to invade their personal items; notice any changes or unusual activity.

- Put up cameras in the common areas and let the employees know.

- Ensure that travel expenses are supported with receipts. Make sure you demand the original receipts and not copies. Review these and make sure there are no unnecessary expenses.

- Employees who steal are always on the lookout for loopholes they can take advantage of. During shift changes, corrupt employees will try to push the cash shortage onto the next employee. Cash register drawers should only be assigned to one employee.

- Surveillance cameras are useful for monitoring the cash register drawers and to catch employees stealing.

- Test your employees by placing extra cash in the cash drawer; it will give you the opportunity to test the morals of the person.

- Consistent bookkeeping reviews can tell the real financial position of a small business. Analysis should constantly and continuously be done, and any discrepancies in cash and goods must be noticed, marked down, and followed up to see where it went missing. Have tangible evidence of theft before filing a police report.

To prevent future theft, file charges against the thief and prosecute them. That will be a message to others. If you look the other way, an employee who "is down on their luck and only needs a temporary loan" isn't going to stop any other employees from stealing. Employee theft is a major problem to small business and accounts for 8 times more than shoplifting.

THROW THE THIEF OUT THE DOOR

How to treat theft:

- Gather evidence - You need to have proof. Gather all documentation, whether video, other employees' statements, or written documentation and put them in chronological order.

- Go through your books and records – You need to either do this yourself or have someone else do it. Review the transactions and understand who the payments are going to, know who you pay. There are numerous cases where the employee has created a fake company that they control and have cleaned out many small businesses.

- Document the theft – If you find anything, create files and document every instance.

- Interview – A thief is usually a good liar, accusing them of theft won't phase a good thief, they've been through it before, be prepared to show your evidence.

- Don't tip them off until you are ready. Even if they get tipped off, more than likely the temptation is too much, and they will continue stealing.

- Document everything – The thief will usually not go away easily. With the documentation, have other employees provide recorded statements, and compile and document all other evidence that you might need in a prosecution or future lawsuit. This documentation will be valuable if they try to file a claim of disability or unemployment. If you can show the theft they will be denied, so documentation is important.

- Terminate them – Do not keep an employee that is taking you to the cleaners, even on a small level because it is just a reason to continue to steal and shows that an employee stealing from you is ok.

- Get them off the property – Walk them back to their desk, and watch as they clean out their workstation, and then escort them out of the building and off the property.

- Call the police – If they took enough, prosecute. But you must know that the probability of getting any money back is slim.

- Don't deduct the theft from their check – There are laws that prevent this.

- Change the passwords and security codes for the alarm – Keep them out of the computer system as well as the building.

- Take them off any account that they were associated with. Ensure all security changes and that they no longer have any access.

- Backup your system – Don't give them the opportunity for revenge.

These steps may not all be necessary. It doesn't make sense to prosecute an employee for taking office supplies, but you need to be aware and monitor and catch the ones that are stealing from you. It is the owner's business and money, and the most important thing is to protect the company assets and keep the money in the owner's pocket.

What is the point of the book?

This book is designed to give insight and understanding into why Operators succeed, and the good guys fail in small business. It also provides you with actionable strategies to explode your business and bring in gobs of cash that flows into your pockets, doubling, tripling or more your profits. The more time you put in, the better your results will be. One simple strategy or executed tactic could make you millions. This book is not written for entertainment purposes, but is packed with real-life examples, strategies, and tools that can revolutionize your business and catapult you past the competition.

Most importantly, you must gain insight, understanding, tactics or strategy, and EXECUTE.

While you are reading, if you see an example that could possibly tie to your situation, modify, and adapt it as necessary and implement. Don't think – "Well, that doesn't matter". You must execute one, two or more strategies or tactics. They won't all work for every situation, but you must try some as opposed to just reading them. It only takes one or two strategies or tactics, and your business will explode with buckets of additional cash with virtually no more effort or time. All is moot if you fail to act.

Don't be afraid to modify or customize the ideas, opportunities, and strategies so they better fit your specific situation. The most important aspect for your business success is to execute. This book functions as a manual for business. In this book, you can get specific strategies for individual situations.

Warning - when you first try something new, it is usually uncomfortable initially and you might not feel like continuing. However, the more strategies and tactics you employ, and the more you try these out, the easier it becomes. This is much like the old phrase that says, "throw enough sh*t against the wall and something will stick."

Why do aggressive businesspeople succeed? Are they smarter? No, they just don't care what other people think of them. They always look out for number one. If you're not looking out for number one, then who is? No one! You are your own responsibility. It's easy to get caught up in a daily routine, but you'll only get the same results and will never break through. This is your opportunity to have a business breakthrough and get what you deserve. Make your business do the heavy lifting.

To do so, you will need to stretch yourself out of your comfort zone and apply the strategies, tactics, and ideas. It might not work the first time, but if you adjust and modify while continuing to act and keeping your eyes on the goal, you will break through.

I once heard a story about Tim Ferris, a podcaster. When Tim was starting out in college, he was an introvert. He didn't take as much action as he could because he was uncomfortable doing so. However, one day, he made himself do some crazy things to break through. Tim would go into a Starbucks and sit or lay down on the floor in front of the counter for a few minutes. People would ask him if he was OK, and he would say yes. After a while, he would get up and order. The reason he did this was to make himself feel nervous and uncomfortable, as a mental training exercise. This helped him realize his mind could still function in such a state and led to him being able to take more risks and succeed.

Like many of the aggressive businesspeople you encounter in life, you also need to step beyond your comfort zone. Do the uncomfortable, even if your workers, family, customers, and your Facebook friends are calling you stupid for doing new things with your life or business. If you want to maximize your potential, you need to persevere, even when it's uncomfortable. Not everything will work, and you need thick skin sometimes to keep taking actions towards your goals.

You must select a target (goal, short and long term) and act. You must hold yourself accountable on a weekly basis. If you can make the necessary adjustments, not only trying the strategies and tactics but also, customizing them as necessary, you will achieve the success you deserve, and the money will flow to you in avalanches of abundance.

Let's get down to business. This book, which is really an operation manual, contains hundreds of ideas, concepts, and strategies that were refined through hundreds of years of combined experience. In this book, we refer to the people with such enormous experience and success as "Business

Operators." Combined, these people have lost 100's of thousands of dollars through trial and error, so that you can make millions. Learn from their mistakes and only grab the wins. Heed the knowledge, but more importantly, act! If you only execute one, two, three, or four strategies, you could easily double, triple, or more your cash flow, profits, and lifestyle.

In today's business environment, where everyone is carrying a computer in their pocket, it is easy to be distracted and never get anything done. The Operators use the phone as a tool and don't let it use them! Let the other so-called businesspeople waste their life away on their Smartphone, while you are crushing the market. Maximize your opportunity; you only have one life and one chance – make the most of it.

WHAT QUALITIES DOES THE OPERATORS POSSESS?

The first trait is that they do not care what others think about them. They have thick skin and are not afraid to be embarrassed or fail. Deep down, they have faith in their resilience and that they will ultimately succeed. They also are willing to do whatever it takes to get the job done. In today's market, it seems as though there are three types of small businesspeople.

The first is the multi-level marketer. Their goal is to get someone else to do the work while they get rich doing nothing. The second one is the hard worker, who puts the time in but can never get ahead. They keep doing things but just can't break through. It's not their fault; they lack the education, expertise, or the right opportunity. If they can get the right idea or opportunity and follow through, they can break through.

The third one is a little different. 47% of all small business owners do their own marketing. Where do they learn how to do marketing? From their competitors and what the people did before them. For a small business owner to break through like the third type of Operators, they must get the education and tools to innovate to achieve better results for their time and money. The Operators will find out what the successful businesses do but won't always follow their lead. They get educated and see what works in the market and combine these successful strategies with new ideas and concepts relevant to their own business. They will monitor the results and adjust, until they can create momentum and are able to maximize the business and stuff money in their pocket.

What stops the hard worker from getting the same success? They fear that it won't work, that they are not good enough, that they won't succeed. This keeps them from getting out of their comfort zone and from doing the little things that can add up to important things. I can assure you the smart Operators does not care about all the extraneous noise from people in their business, family, or friends. They know that not everything will work but the one or two that do, will change their business life. They also live outside their comfort zone and push themselves even when it's difficult.

They find strategies that are effective for someone else and apply those to their situation. Yes, it might not work but that is ok, they will try another, and another, and another until they achieve the success they desire.

Operators are not always efficient, they are effective. It is hard to be both.

Bottom line: You get what you "tolerate", and as they say, "nice guys finish last."

CONCLUDE

Overall, breaking the barriers is all about finding work for you to be successful. Oftentimes, we try to look at others around us or on tv and try to imagine what success feels like or how they got to the top. The important key thing to remember is to never give up because of one alternative or even multiple, there is always a way, if there is a will. My parents always reminded me of that statement and after accomplishing all the success I've had so far in both personally and career I continue to remember that anything is truly possible if you put your mind to it. This is my first book of many, and I felt the need to inspire both the young and older business owners that you can start any day with any idea and turn it into success. Having mentors and supporters around you that supports your best interest is something I'm grateful for. God has blessed me in countless ways and to be able to give back a piece of what I've been given is important because it helps the next person when it's their time to break through to success. Next time you're around people that you believe are successful in their eyes, ask them questions about how they got there and the ways they continue to stay successful. One thing I learned from my post college career after graduating from University of Notre Dame, is that nothing is guaranteed and if you do have any success in the professional world, it will be 10x times harder to stay at the top. Sometimes people have a false narrative on what they believe successful people do to stay successful and that's work extremely hard to continue breaking through the barriers of success. We covered various topics and ways for one to breakthrough and take risks, having a plan, and executing is something we can all take from reading this book that it's essential. If you have read the book and still are not sure of ways you can break through, be sure to reach out to me and we can get a game plan on how to take it to the next level. Go out and chase after your dreams, make the tough choices that it will take to be successful but once you get a taste of what it feels like, you become addicted to wanting to be successful. Which is why you see the hardest workers the most successful in their daily lives because to do something that only very few accomplish, one must know it's going to take an extreme level of demanding work, dedication, and love for what you're doing.

From my own experience, I kept God first and put my head down and worked hard knowing that one day I will graduate from a prestigious college and play in the NFL. Listening to my parent's harp on being a diligent worker and knowing how to face adversity gave me the tools to be able to take experiences I learned through being raised and playing sports growing up. I want the success for you, which is why I authored this novel with MJ to discuss ways to break through the barriers of success and using the knowledge you already must create. You can apply these same tools to anything you want to be in life, and you will find yourself enjoying it and having success at the same time. From this day forward after reading this book, promise me when barriers come, you will find a solution and the continuous of hard-work has to be a tool that's used daily. Success will never be easy, and if one has ever told you that it will be, they were mistaken because getting to the top is hard but staying at the top is harder and relying on your training and natural ability will give you the best chances. Remember, take risk to get things you dream of having, and understand what you have is more enough to create more, which will compound over time and eventually you will have more than enough. Can you image? Carpe diem.

AFTERWORD

"Don't be distracted by criticism. Remember–the only taste of success some people get is to take a bite out of you." — Zig Ziglar

For more information or get involved with us reach out to Jan Capital Inc. www.jancapitalinc.com

Made in the USA
Monee, IL
15 November 2022